FEMALE

*The Masculine Triad and Her Fight
for Freedom and Independence*

— A Prosecution —

First Edition

ISBN: 979-8-9943268-0-0

CONTENTS

The Case for Female Freedom

Members of the jury, esteemed colleagues, and witnesses to history:

We gather here today to examine a case that spans millennia, crosses continents, and touches the lives of every woman who has ever lived. This is not merely a historical inquiry, nor is it simply an academic exercise. This is a prosecution—a methodical presentation of evidence demonstrating that the Female has been systematically denied the very freedoms that her oppressors have claimed as their unalienable birthright.

The defendant in this case is not a single individual, but rather a triumvirate of power that has collaborated, whether intentionally or circumstantially, to restrict female autonomy, control female bodies, limit female movement, and deny female independence throughout human history. I call this alliance the **Masculine Triad**: God, Devil, and Man.

Before you recoil at the audacity of this framework, let us examine the evidence with clear eyes and rational minds. Each member of this Triad has demonstrated, through word and deed, an unwavering commitment to their own freedom and independence. Each has fought for, claimed, or demanded sovereignty. And yet, when the Female seeks that same freedom, she is met with resistance, punishment, and condemnation from all three.

The Triad's Claims to Freedom

God, as presented in the biblical narrative, asserts absolute sovereignty. He is all-powerful, all-knowing, and demands worship and obedience from His creation. His very nature is freedom incarnate—He answers to no one, constrains to no authority, and declares: "I AM WHO I AM." This is the ultimate expression of independence. God requires submission from all beings, yet submits to none. His position is inherently that of complete, unqualified freedom.

The Devil, also known as Lucifer or Satan, waged war for his independence. According to Christian tradition, he refused to serve, refused to submit, and fought against God Himself for autonomy. Though he lost this battle and was cast from Heaven, his rebellion was fundamentally a fight for freedom—a declaration that he would rather rule in Hell than serve in Heaven. The Devil's entire mythology rests on his quest for self-determination, his refusal to accept a subordinate position, his insistence on independence.

Man, throughout recorded history, has fought countless wars, toppled governments, penned declarations, and spilled rivers of blood— all in the name of freedom and independence. The American Declaration of Independence proclaims it "self-evident, that all men are created equal, that they are endowed by their Creator with certain unalienable Rights, that among these are Life, Liberty and the pursuit of Happiness." Men have outlawed slavery (of other men), established democracies (for men), and created constitutions guaranteeing rights (to men). Man's struggle for freedom is documented, celebrated, and enshrined in the collective consciousness of civilization.

The Question Before Us

Given this evidence—that God claims absolute sovereignty, that the Devil fought for independence, and that Man has waged perpetual war for freedom—one question arises with devastating clarity:

Why is it considered unthinkable, unnatural, or impermissible for the Female to desire and fight for her own Freedom and Independence?

This question is not rhetorical. It demands an answer. And as we proceed through the evidence, you will find that the only consistent answer across time, culture, and ideology is this: **because each member of the Masculine Triad has a vested interest in maintaining control over the Female.**

The Pattern of Oppression

Throughout history, we will demonstrate that:

- **God** has designated the Female as subordinate, cursed her uniquely, and established religious doctrines that mandate her submission

- **The Devil** has manipulated, deceived, and demonized the Female, using her as a scapegoat while simultaneously being blamed for teaching her forbidden knowledge

- **Man** has enslaved, raped, beaten, bought, sold, silenced, and legally erased the Female, all while claiming his own freedom as a natural right

The evidence will show that when one member of the Triad oppresses the Female, the others do not intervene—they collaborate. When God curses Eve with painful childbirth and subordination to her husband, Man enforces these "divine" mandates through law and custom. When the Devil is blamed for teaching women witchcraft, both God's church and Man's courts burn her at the stake. When Man enslaves and brutalizes women, religious authorities cite God's word to justify it, while simultaneously attributing female sexuality and independence to the Devil's influence.

This is not coincidence. This is pattern. This is system. This is the Masculine Triad.

The Scope of This Inquiry

The case I present today will proceed chronologically, beginning in the Garden of Eden and progressing through ancient civilizations, medieval darkness, the age of Enlightenment, and into our contemporary moment. We will examine:

- **Biblical and religious texts** that established female subordination as divinely ordained

- **Historical facts** documenting the legal, economic, and physical subjugation of women

- **Folklore and mythology** that shaped cultural attitudes toward female autonomy

- **Laws and customs** that restricted female movement, speech, property, and personhood

- **Violence and exploitation** perpetrated against women across cultures and centuries

• **Resistance and progress** demonstrating the Female's persistent fight for freedom

Each piece of evidence will be presented as it occurred in the timeline of human history, allowing you to see how the pattern evolved, adapted, and persisted across vastly different contexts. Some examples will be familiar—the story of Eve, the witch trials, the suffrage movement. Others may be less known but equally powerful in demonstrating the systematic nature of female oppression.

The Standard of Evidence

I do not ask you to accept these claims on emotion alone. I present facts. I cite sources. I build a case as any competent attorney would: piece by piece, witness by witness, document by document. Where religious texts are invoked, I quote them directly. Where historical events are discussed, I provide context and corroboration. Where cultural practices are examined, I demonstrate their global reach and persistent nature.

Some may argue that conditions have improved, that progress has been made, that modern women have freedoms their ancestors could not imagine. This is true. But the question is not whether progress has occurred—it is whether that progress was granted willingly or extracted through struggle. The answer, as the evidence will demonstrate, is the latter. Every freedom women possess today was fought for, bled for, and won against fierce resistance from the Masculine Triad.

The Thesis

After presenting this extensive body of evidence, I will demonstrate conclusively that:

The Female fight for Freedom and Independence is as valid, legitimate, and honorable as any fight for freedom undertaken by God (who claimed it), by the Devil (who warred for it), or by Man (who has secured it for himself). The Masculine Triad has no innate, natural, or legal right, nor honest argument to the contrary.

This is not a call for revenge. This is not an indictment of all men or a rejection of all religion. This is simply a demand for consistency. If freedom is self-evident for males, it must be self-evident for females. If independence is a natural right for one, it is a natural right for all. If the Devil himself could fight for autonomy and be remembered in epic terms, surely the Female can do the same without being branded as evil, selfish, or unnatural.

A Note on Method

This book is structured to present evidence methodically and allow you, the reader, to reach your own conclusions based on the facts. I do not ask you to take my word for anything—I ask you to examine the evidence. Look at what God said and did. Look at what the Devil is credited with. Look at what Man has enacted into law and practiced as custom. Then ask yourself: Is the Female's desire for freedom really so unreasonable? Or has it simply been made to appear so by those who benefit from her subjugation?

We will proceed through four major eras:

Part I: The Foundation of the Triad will examine how the subordination of the Female was established from the very beginning, in religious texts and ancient civilizations.

Part II: The Medieval Triad will document the darkest period of female oppression, when witchcraft accusations and religious authority combined to murder thousands of independent women.

Part III: The Modern Triad will reveal the bitter irony of the Enlightenment and subsequent "ages of reason," during which men fought for freedom while systematically excluding women.

Part IV: The Contemporary Triad will bring us to the present day, examining both the progress made and the resistance that persists, while looking toward a future where female freedom need not be perpetually justified.

The Journey Ahead

What follows is not comfortable reading. It will challenge cherished beliefs. It will present familiar stories in unfamiliar light. It will ask you to see patterns you may have previously dismissed or overlooked. But I promise you this: every claim will be supported, every assertion will be grounded in evidence, and the conclusion will be inescapable.

The Female has been denied freedom by those who claim it for themselves. She has been subjugated by those who fight against subjugation. She has been told that her desire for autonomy is selfish, unnatural, and destructive—by entities whose entire existence is predicated on their own autonomy.

This ends now. Not with anger, but with evidence. Not with accusation, but with documentation. Not with emotion, but with fact.

Ladies and gentlemen, let us examine the evidence.

PART I: THE FOUNDATION OF THE TRIAD

The Garden of Eden — The Original Trap

"In the beginning..."

Every story has an origin, and the origin of female subjugation begins in a garden. For billions of people across thousands of years, the story of Adam and Eve has been the foundational narrative explaining the relationship between man and woman, between humanity and God, between obedience and consequence. It is taught to children, preached from pulpits, and embedded in the cultural consciousness of Western civilization and beyond.

But let us examine this origin story not as parable or moral lesson, but as our first piece of evidence. Let us look at what actually happened in Eden, who said what to whom, and what the consequences reveal about the Masculine Triad's treatment of the Female from the very beginning.

The Derivative Creation

The Book of Genesis provides two accounts of human creation, but it is the second account—the one involving the rib—that has most profoundly shaped attitudes toward women. Let us read the text:

> *"Then the Lord God caused a deep sleep to fall upon the man, and while he slept took one of his ribs and closed up its place with flesh. And the rib that the Lord God had taken from the man he made into a woman and brought her to the man." (Genesis 2:21-22)*

Consider what this narrative establishes: Woman is not created independently, from the same raw material as Man (dust of the earth). She is created from Man, as a derivative of Man, for the purpose of serving Man. Even the terminology reveals the hierarchy—she is "built" (the Hebrew word *banah*) from Adam's side, while Adam was "formed" (Hebrew *yatsar*) by God directly from earth.

God Himself describes the purpose of this creation:

> *"Then the Lord God said, 'It is not good that the man should be alone; I will make him a helper fit for him.'" (Genesis 2:18)*

A **helper**. Not an equal companion. Not an independent being. Not a co-ruler of creation. A helper. The Hebrew word *ezer kenegdo* is often translated as "helper suitable for him" or "helper corresponding to him." Centuries of religious teaching have insisted this does not imply inferiority, that the word *ezer* is also used for God helping humans. But context matters. God helps humans from a position of superior power. In Eden, the hierarchy is clear: Adam names the woman (just as he named the animals, demonstrating dominion), and she is explicitly created to solve Adam's problem of loneliness.

> ***Evidence for the Prosecution***: *From the moment of her creation, the Female was positioned as subordinate and derivative. She was not given a choice about her existence, her purpose, or her relationship to Man. This was God's design, the first act of the Masculine Triad in controlling Female destiny.*

The Trap is Set

God places one restriction on the first humans:

> *"But of the tree of the knowledge of good and evil you shall not eat, for in the day that you eat of it you shall surely die." (Genesis 2:17)*

This command was given to Adam before Eve's creation. She learns of it second-hand, likely through Adam. Already we see the pattern: God speaks to Man, Man mediates to Woman. The direct line of communication runs through the masculine.

Now enters the second member of our Triad: the Devil, in the form of the serpent.

The text tells us the serpent was "more crafty than any other beast of the field which the Lord God had made" (Genesis 3:1). The serpent approaches Eve—not Adam, though many scholars note Adam may have been present. The serpent asks:

> *"Did God actually say, 'You shall not eat of any tree in the garden'?" (Genesis 3:1)*

Eve corrects the serpent, demonstrating she knows the rule, but adds a detail not in God's original command: "neither shall you touch it, lest you die" (Genesis 3:3). Whether this was Adam's embellishment or Eve's own addition, we cannot know. But the serpent challenges God's word:

> *"You will not surely die. For God knows that when you eat of it your eyes will be opened, and you will be like God, knowing good and evil." (Genesis 3:4-5)*

> ***Evidence for the Prosecution****: The Devil targets Female for deception. Whether because she is perceived as more susceptible, more easily isolated, or more likely to influence Adam, the choice is deliberate. The Devil uses her as the instrument through which to challenge God's authority. She is manipulated by the second member of the Triad.*

Eve, seeing that "the tree was good for food, and that it was a delight to the eyes, and that the tree was to be desired to make one wise," eats the fruit. Then—and this detail is crucial—"she also gave some to her husband who was with her, and he ate" (Genesis 3:6).

Adam was there. He watched. He ate. He made his own choice.

The Consequences: Unequal Judgment

When God discovers their disobedience, He questions them. Note the order: God calls to Adam first. "Where are you?" God asks the man, not the woman. Adam's response is telling:

"The woman whom you gave to be with me, she gave me fruit of the tree, and I ate." (Genesis 3:12)

Evidence for the Prosecution: *Man immediately blames the Female. He does not take responsibility for his own choice. He points to the woman—emphasizing that God Himself gave her to him, thus sharing some blame—and only at the end admits his own action. This is Man's first recorded act after the fall: deflection of responsibility onto the Female, establishing a pattern that would persist for millennia.*

Eve, when questioned, says: "The serpent deceived me, and I ate" (Genesis 3:13). She admits deception and her action. But note: both of them ate willingly, yet the punishments are strikingly different.

God curses the serpent first, condemning it to crawl and eat dust. Then He pronounces the consequences for Eve:

"I will surely multiply your pain in childbearing; in pain you shall bring forth children. Your desire shall be for your husband, and he shall rule over you." (Genesis 3:16)

Let us examine this carefully. The Female receives a dual punishment:

1. **Physical pain in childbirth** - A burden Man will never experience, a pain inflicted specifically on the female body for the act of bringing life into the world. The very process that perpetuates humanity becomes torturous.

2. **Subordination to her husband** - "He shall rule over you." This is not presented as existing hierarchy made explicit; religious scholars argue over whether Adam had authority before this moment. But the text is clear: whatever the relationship was before, it is now codified that Man will rule over Woman. Her desire will be for her husband, yet he will have authority over her.

Compare this to Adam's punishment:

"Cursed is the ground because of you; in pain you shall eat of it all the days of your life; thorns and thistles it shall bring forth for you... By the sweat of your face you shall eat bread, till you return to the ground, for out of it you were taken; for you are dust, and to dust you shall return." (Genesis 3:17-19)

Adam's punishment is hard work. Agricultural labor. Mortality. These are universal human conditions—women also must work, must eat by effort, must die. But Adam does not receive a punishment targeting his body specifically for his sex. He does not receive a punishment making him subordinate to another human being. He receives hardship, but not subjugation.

> ***Evidence for the Prosecution****: God punishes Female more severely and in ways that specifically restrict her autonomy. Physical pain in her unique biological function, and social subordination to Man. The groundwork for female oppression is laid by God Himself, in the very first pages of human history.*

The Expulsion: Collective Punishment, Individual Blame

After pronouncing judgment, God expels both Adam and Eve from Eden. He places cherubim with a flaming sword to guard the way back, ensuring they cannot eat from the tree of life and live forever.

They are both expelled. They will both toil. They will both die. But the cultural and religious memory of this event does not equally distribute the blame.

Throughout subsequent millennia, Eve has been held as primarily responsible for humanity's fall. Church fathers like Tertullian would call women "the devil's gateway" and "the first deserter of the divine law." Augustine would develop the doctrine of original sin, transmitted through reproduction—through woman's body. In art, literature, and sermon, Eve is the temptress, the weak one, the foolish one who doomed humanity.

Adam, meanwhile, is often portrayed as having been led astray. His sin is following his wife. His punishment is having to deal with her sin's consequences. The narrative consistently shifts greater blame onto the Female.

> ***Evidence for the Prosecution***: *All three members of the*
> *Masculine Triad participate in Female's subjugation in Eden:*
> - ***God*** *creates her as subordinate, curses her*
>   *uniquely, and establishes male rule over her*
> - ***The Devil*** *uses her as his instrument,*
>   *deceiving her and ensuring eternal enmity*
>   *between serpent and woman*
> - ***Man*** *blames her, and then benefits from the*
>   *divine mandate that he shall rule over her*

The Original Questions

Let us pause and ask several questions that will resonate throughout our case:

Why did God create Eve from Adam's rib, rather than equally from dust?

The standard religious answer is to show their unity, that they are "one flesh." But this explanation conveniently ignores that unity could have been established without hierarchy. Two beings created equally from dust could still become one flesh in marriage. The derivative creation establishes, from the very beginning, that Woman comes from Man, is made for Man, is secondary to Man.

Why did the Devil target Eve?

Whether one believes this literally or metaphorically, the choice is significant. Either the Devil perceived Eve as more susceptible (suggesting inherent female weakness, a claim that would echo through centuries), or he recognized that influencing Eve would be the most effective way to reach Adam (suggesting her role as helper/ influencer), or Adam was standing right there and equally responsible (suggesting the scapegoating of Eve is unjust). None of these options reflect well on the Masculine Triad.

Why did God punish Eve with subordination to Adam, rather than punishing them equally?

If both sinned, both should face equal consequences. But they didn't. Eve's punishment includes being placed under Adam's rule. This is social control, not natural consequence. It is God establishing patriarchy as divine punishment.

Why did Adam immediately blame Eve?

Because he could. Because the system would support him. Because deflecting responsibility onto the Female was already, in that moment, the path of least resistance. And he was right—history largely did blame her.

The Pattern Established

The Eden narrative establishes several patterns that will repeat throughout our case:

1. **Female is created for male purposes, not as an independent being**

2. **Female is held to different standards and faces harsher consequences**

3. **Male authority over the Female is presented as divinely ordained**

4. **Female is blamed disproportionately, even when Male is equally culpable**

5. **Female's desire for knowledge and autonomy is characterized as sin**

That last point deserves emphasis. What was Eve's sin? She desired wisdom. She wanted to "be like God, knowing good and evil." This desire for knowledge, for transcendence, for something more than her assigned role—this is framed as the original sin. The message is clear: Female must not aspire beyond her station. She must not seek knowledge independently. She must not desire what God and Man have reserved for themselves.

> *Evidence for the Prosecution: The Eden story is not merely describing what happened; it is prescribing what should happen. It is establishing the template for male authority and female subordination. It is teaching, generation after generation, that this hierarchy is natural, divinely ordained, and the consequence of Female's inherent weakness and sinfulness.*

The Defense That Cannot Stand

Religious apologists offer various defenses of this narrative:

"The curse was consequence, not prescription—it describes what sin brought into the world, not what should be."

And yet, for thousands of years, religious authorities have used this text to prescribe female submission. They haven't said "We should work to overcome the curse of Eden." They've said "Submit, because God ordained male rule as your punishment." When used for millennia as prescription, consequence becomes indistinguishable from command.

"The pain in childbirth and male authority were exaggerations of what already existed, not entirely new conditions."

Even if we accept this (and the text doesn't clearly state it), the question remains: Why? Why would a just God exaggerate female suffering specifically? Why not equally exaggerate male consequences? Why is female-specific pain and subordination the chosen form of punishment?

"Adam and Eve were equal before the fall; hierarchy came only after."

This makes it worse, not better. It means God's response to human sin was to create inequality where none existed before. It means patriarchy is explicitly divine punishment. It means every act of female subjugation since then can claim divine mandate. How is this a defense?

"This is just one interpretation; other readings are possible."

Indeed, other readings are possible, and some modern religious scholars offer more egalitarian interpretations. But for the vast majority of human history, the dominant interpretation—the one that shaped law, custom, and culture—was clear: Woman is subordinate to Man because God said so. The interpretation that matters is the one that was enacted into the world.

The Lasting Impact

The Eden narrative accomplished something profound: it placed the origin of female subjugation at the origin of humanity itself. It made patriarchy not a human invention, but a divine decree. It made female pain not an injustice to be corrected, but a curse to be endured.

Every subsequent restriction on female freedom would point back to Eden. Every denial of female independence would cite Eve's weakness. Every enforcement of male authority would invoke God's curse. The garden became the eternal justification for temporal oppression.

And the three members of the Masculine Triad all played their roles:

- **God** designed and enforced the hierarchy

- **The Devil** provided the occasion and took his share of blame (while simultaneously being credited with "teaching" Eve to think independently)

- Man benefited from the arrangement and blamed the Female for his own choices

The First Link in the Chain

The Garden of Eden is not merely a story. It is not merely mythology. It is the foundation upon which thousands of years of female subjugation would be built. It is the first piece of evidence in a case that spans continents and centuries.

A woman was created to serve. She was deceived by one member of the Triad, blamed by another, and cursed by the third. She was then expelled from paradise and told that pain and subordination would be her lot.

And when, throughout history, women would ask "Why?"—why must we suffer this, why must we submit, why can't we have the freedom and independence that men claim—the answer would always circle back to a garden, a serpent, and a piece of fruit.

The trap was set in Eden. The rest of history would spring it shut.

> ***Evidence for the Prosecution****: The foundation of female subordination was laid by the Masculine Triad in the Garden of Eden, establishing a divine mandate for patriarchy that would justify millennia of oppression.*

The case continues in Chapter 2, where we examine how ancient civilizations built legal and social systems upon this foundation, transforming the Female from deity to property.

CHAPTER TWO

Ancient Mesopotamia and Egypt — Goddess to Property

From the divine to the disposable

The Garden of Eden established the theological foundation for female subordination. But theology alone does not create civilization— it must be enacted into law, embedded into custom, and enforced through institutions. In this chapter, we examine how ancient Mesopotamia and Egypt transformed the mythological subordination of women into legal and social reality.

Here we witness a profound and tragic transition: from female deities worshipped as the most powerful forces in the universe, to women treated as property under the law. This shift did not happen overnight, nor was it inevitable. It was deliberate, systematic, and supported by all three members of the Masculine Triad.

The Goddess Era: When Female Power Was Divine

Before we examine how women became property, we must acknowledge what was lost.

In the earliest civilizations of Mesopotamia—Sumer, Akkad, Babylon—the most powerful deities were often female. **Inanna** (later called **Ishtar**) was the Queen of Heaven, goddess of love, war, fertility, justice, and political power. She was not a gentle, nurturing figure relegated to the domestic sphere. She was fierce, independent, sexual, and commanding.

Inanna descended to the underworld and returned. She defied her own sister, the Queen of the Dead. She was worshipped by both men and women, served by priests of both sexes. In the Epic of Gilgamesh, when the hero-king rejects her marriage proposal, she unleashes the Bull of Heaven upon his city—demonstrating her power over life and death, her refusal to be spurned, her divine autonomy.

***Evidence for the Prosecution**: In the earliest written records of human civilization (circa 4000-3000 BCE), female power was not only acknowledged—it was worshipped. Women could embody divine authority, sexual freedom, martial strength, and political sovereignty. The female was not inherently subordinate in these religious systems.*

Similarly, in Egypt, the goddess **Isis** was among the most powerful deities, associated with magic, healing, motherhood, and resurrection. She recovered the scattered pieces of her murdered husband Osiris and brought him back to life—a demonstration of female power over death itself. Egyptian mythology featured numerous powerful goddesses: Hathor, Sekhmet, Ma'at, Bastet. The divine feminine was not weak, not subordinate, not silent.

This matters profoundly to our case. The claim that female subordination is "natural" or "divinely ordained from the beginning" is contradicted by humanity's own early religious expressions. Before the Masculine Triad consolidated its power, humans worshipped female deities as supreme.

But as civilizations developed, as written law codes emerged, as property became central to social organization, something changed. The goddesses remained in name, but real women lost power. The transition from matriarchal or egalitarian spiritual systems to patriarchal legal systems represents one of history's most consequential shifts.

The Code of Hammurabi: Women as Legal Property

Let us turn to evidence that cannot be disputed: written law.

The **Code of Hammurabi** (circa 1750 BCE) is one of the earliest and most complete legal codes in human history. Carved into a seven-and-a-half-foot stone stele, it was publicly displayed in Babylon so all could know the law. At its top is a relief showing Hammurabi receiving divine authority from the sun god Shamash—establishing that these laws carry religious sanction.

The Code contains 282 laws covering everything from property disputes to family relations, from commercial transactions to criminal punishment. It is often celebrated as an early form of justice, establishing the principle of proportional punishment ("an eye for an eye"). But let us examine what it reveals about the treatment of women.

Women as Property in Marriage

Under Hammurabi's Code, marriage was not a union of equals but a property transaction. A woman "entered into marriage through a contract arranged by her family. She came with a dowry, and the gifts given by the groom to the bride also came with her." The woman herself had little say in this arrangement. Her value was economic, transferable, negotiable.

Law 138 states: "If a free man wishes to divorce his wife who has had no children, he must pay her a settlement equal to the value of the gifts he gave her father when they were married plus the dowry she brought from her father's house; by paying this settlement he divorces her."

Note the structure: The man wishes to divorce. The man pays. The man divorces. The woman is the object of these transactions, not the subject. Her childlessness—her failure to fulfill her primary economic function—justifies his unilateral decision to end the marriage.

Compare this to a woman seeking divorce. Law 142: "If a woman wishes to divorce her husband and refuses him sexual rights, an inquiry shall be held. If she has not committed adultery but her husband has, she may take her dowry and return to her father's house."

Even when the husband is the adulterer, the woman must undergo an inquiry. She must prove her own faithfulness. She must justify her desire for freedom. And if she cannot prove her case? Law 143: "If she has committed adultery, then she shall be executed by being thrown into the water."

Evidence for the Prosecution: The law treats male and female adultery asymmetrically. A man's infidelity might allow his wife to leave with her dowry—if she can prove it, if she can endure the inquiry, if she submits to the process. A woman's adultery is a capital offense.

This is not justice. This is the legal codification of female subordination.

Women as Reproductive Commodities

The Code reveals an obsession with controlling female fertility and ensuring legitimate male heirs. Laws governing pregnancy, childbirth, and children's status are extensive and detailed. Women who fail to produce children are devalued. Women who produce children secure marginally better legal protections. But in all cases, the children belong to the father.

If a man's wife cannot bear children, he may take a second wife or a slave as a concubine. But a woman has no such option—her husband's infertility is not grounds for her to seek another partner. The reproductive burden falls entirely on her, while reproductive freedom belongs entirely to him.

***Evidence for the Prosecution**: Under Hammurabi's Code, a woman's legal status and economic security depend almost entirely on her relationship to men (father, husband, son) and her ability to produce male heirs. She is valued for her reproductive capacity and penalized for its absence.*

The Illusion of Protection

Defenders of Hammurabi's Code note that it provided some protections for women—they could own property in limited circumstances, they could divorce abusive husbands under certain conditions, they had rights to inheritance. This is true. But let us be clear: **these are not rights; these are permissions**. They are granted by male authority and can be revoked by male authority. They exist within a system that fundamentally treats women as property, not persons.

The Code "recognized that women needed certain legal protections from male authority." Why? Because without these protections, the abuse was so severe and so common that it threatened social order. These laws are not evidence of female equality; they are evidence of how desperately protection was needed from male violence and exploitation.

Masculine Triad Actions in Mesopotamian Law:

• God/Religion: Divine authority (Shamash) sanctions the legal code, making patriarchy a matter of sacred law

• Man: Creates and enforces laws that treat women as property, sexually subordinate, and reproductively controlled

• Devil: Would later be blamed for female sexuality and independence, but in this era, the system itself was sufficient to control women

The Lilith Legend: The Demonization of Female Equality

We cannot leave ancient Mesopotamia without examining one of its most revealing legends: the story of **Lilith**.

Though not appearing in the canonical biblical Genesis narrative, Lilith emerges in ancient Jewish folklore as Adam's first wife. According to the *Alphabet of Ben Sira* (circa 8th-10th century CE, but drawing on much earlier Mesopotamian demon mythology), Lilith was created from the earth just as Adam was—not from his rib, but as his equal.

The story tells us that "they immediately began to quarrel." Over what? Sexual position. When Adam demanded that Lilith lie beneath him during intercourse, she refused, stating: "We are equal to each other inasmuch as we were both created from the earth."

Lilith claimed equality. She refused subordination. When Adam would not relent, "Lilith then pronounced the ineffable name of God and flew away" from Eden. God sent three angels to retrieve her, but she refused to return. She told them she would rather accept punishment than submit to Adam's authority.

And so she was demonized. In subsequent mythology, Lilith becomes a child-killer, a seducer of men, a demon of the night who steals male seed and spawns demon babies. Amulets were created to protect infants from her. She was transformed from the first independent woman into the archetypal female monster.

***Evidence for the Prosecution**: When a female figure demands equality with a male figure, refuses subordination, and claims the same creation status, she is not celebrated for asserting her rights. She is demonized, cast out, blamed for child death, and used for millennia as a warning to women: This is what happens when you demand equality.*

The Lilith legend reveals the deep anxiety underlying patriarchal systems: What if women refused subordination? What if they demanded equal status? The answer, according to the legend, is to make an example of her—to ensure every woman who hears the story understands that independence equals monstrosity.

Modern feminist scholars have reclaimed Lilith as "a symbol of autonomy, independence, and sexual liberation." But for thousands of years, she served the opposite purpose: reinforcing the message that female equality was unnatural, dangerous, and deserving of eternal punishment.

> *All three members of the Masculine Triad participate in this demonization:*
>
> - *God: Sends angels to force her return, curses her when she refuses*
>
> - *Adam/Man: Demands subordination, rejects equality, accepts her replacement*
>
> - *Devil/Demon: Lilith herself is recast as demonic, associated with the devil, blamed for harming children and men*

Ancient Egypt: The Exception That Proves the Rule

Let us turn briefly to ancient Egypt, which presents a more complex picture.

Egyptian women enjoyed more legal rights than their Mesopotamian counterparts. They could own property, conduct business, initiate divorce, and inherit estates. Some women even ruled as pharaohs (Hatshepsut, Cleopatra). The goddess Isis was central to Egyptian religion, and female divine power was acknowledged.

Does this contradict our thesis? No—it strengthens it.

First, even in Egypt, women's legal rights were limited compared to men's. Women could own property, but sons inherited over daughters in most cases. Women could rule, but their authority was often questioned or required justification through male lineage. Egyptian queens were powerful, but Egyptian law still privileged male authority.

Second, Egypt demonstrates that patriarchy is not inevitable. It is a choice. When civilizations granted women more autonomy, society did not collapse. The gods did not punish them. Culture flourished. This proves that the restrictions imposed elsewhere were not necessary— they were chosen.

Third, even Egypt's relative egalitarianism eroded over time. As Egypt came under Greek and later Roman rule, women's rights contracted. The pattern repeats: when patriarchal systems consolidate power, female autonomy shrinks.

> ***Evidence for the Prosecution****: The fact that some ancient societies granted women more rights than others demonstrates that female subordination was not natural, inevitable, or divinely required. It was a deliberate choice made by societies and enforced through law.*

The Pattern Established: From Goddess to Property

Let us summarize what has occurred in this chapter:

In the earliest civilizations, female deities were worshipped as supreme powers—gods of war, love, fertility, justice, resurrection. Female power was acknowledged, revered, and central to religious life.

As written law developed, this religious acknowledgment did not translate into social reality. Women were increasingly defined by their relationships to men and their reproductive capacity. Law codes like Hammurabi's treated women as property—valuable property, perhaps, deserving of some protection, but property nonetheless.

Legends like Lilith's served to demonize female independence and equality, ensuring that the theological foundation laid in Eden was reinforced through cultural narrative: women who demand equality are monsters.

Even in societies like Egypt where women enjoyed more rights, male authority remained dominant, and those rights eroded under outside influence.

The transition was complete: Female deity worship did not protect real women from legal subordination. The goddesses remained in temples; women became chattel in courts.

> *Evidence for the Prosecution: Ancient Mesopotamian and Egyptian civilizations transformed the mythological subordination established in Genesis into legal and social reality. Through written law, women were defined as property, controlled reproductively, denied equality, and punished more harshly than men for the same offenses. When women asserted equality (as in the Lilith legend), they were demonized as warnings to others.*

The Masculine Triad's Role:

> • **God/Religion**: Divine sanction was invoked for legal codes that treated women as property; female figures who demanded equality were cast as demons

> • **Man**: Created and enforced laws systematically subordinating women; reduced them from worshipped deities to legal property

> • **Devil**: Used in legends (Lilith) to demonize female independence; would later be blamed for teaching women forbidden knowledge female independence; would later be blamed

The Foundation Is Set

We have now witnessed two foundational moments in the systematic subordination of women:

In Chapter 1, we saw how the Eden narrative established female subordination as divinely ordained—woman created for man, cursed for her disobedience, placed under male rule.

In this chapter, we have seen how ancient civilizations transformed that theological foundation into legal reality—women literally became property under written law, their autonomy restricted, their equality denied.

The foundation is set. The pattern is established. As we move forward through history, we will see this pattern repeat and intensify: religious justification combined with legal enforcement, cultural narratives warning against female independence, and resistance met with punishment.

The Masculine Triad has built its case. Now we see how it was enforced.

In Chapter 3, we turn to ancient Greece and Rome—the birthplace of Western democracy and philosophy, where men fought for freedom while explicitly excluding women from its benefits.

CHAPTER THREE

Ancient Greece and Rome — Democracy for Men Only

The birthplace of freedom, for half the population

We arrive now at one of history's most profound ironies. Ancient Greece and Rome are celebrated as the foundational civilizations of Western democracy, philosophy, and law. They gave us concepts of citizenship, individual rights, and political participation. They fought wars against tyranny, penned treatises on liberty, and erected monuments to freedom.

And they excluded women from all of it.

Not incidentally. Not as an oversight. Not as a temporary condition awaiting reform. They excluded women systematically, philosophically, and—most damningly—while simultaneously creating the very language and concepts of democracy and human rights.

This chapter examines how the civilizations that invented "freedom" for men simultaneously codified subordination for women, and how the intellectual giants who shaped Western thought devoted considerable effort to philosophically justifying female inferiority.

Athens: The Cradle of Democracy's Hypocrisy

The word "democracy" comes from ancient Greek: *demos* (people) and *kratos* (rule). Rule of the people. When Athenian democracy emerged in the 5th century BCE, it was revolutionary—citizens could participate directly in government, vote on laws, serve on juries, and hold public office.

But who counted as "the people"?

Adult male Athenian citizens—and only them. Women, slaves, freed slaves, children, and foreign residents were excluded from citizenship and all political participation. Only about 20 percent of Athens's population were citizens, meaning 80% of people living in this "democracy" had no voice in how it was governed.

> ***Evidence for the Prosecution****: When Athenians invented democracy, they explicitly defined it to exclude women. This was not an accident of history or a gradual development—it was the foundational design.*

The exclusion was total and systematic. Women could not vote, could not speak in the assembly, could not hold office, could not serve on juries, and were excluded from the demes (the basic units of political organization). They were rarely permitted out in public and were even restricted as to where they could be within their own homes.

Under Pericles in 450 BCE, citizenship requirements were tightened further: a citizen had to be born to an Athenian father *and* an

Athenian mother. This created the peculiar legal situation where women were necessary for producing citizens but could not themselves be citizens in any meaningful political sense. Women had citizenship status for purposes of marriage and inheritance but were barred from exercising any of the rights that made citizenship valuable.

As the contemporary Greek historian Thucydides wrote, reflecting Athenian values: "We alone consider a citizen who does not partake in politics not only one who minds his own business but useless." Yet women, by law and custom, could not partake in politics. The logical conclusion: women were "useless" as citizens, valuable only as mothers of male citizens.

> ***Evidence for the Prosecution****: Athens created a system where political participation was the defining characteristic of citizenship and human value, then systematically denied women any possibility of participating. The message was clear: women were not fully human in the way that mattered.*

The Philosophical Justification: Aristotle's "Incomplete Males"

It is one thing for a society to exclude women through custom or convenience. It is another thing entirely for its greatest philosophers—the men whose works would shape Western thought for millennia—to provide elaborate intellectual justifications for that exclusion.

Enter Aristotle (384-322 BCE), student of Plato, tutor of Alexander the Great, and one of the most influential thinkers in human history. Aristotle devoted considerable effort to explaining why women were naturally inferior to men and why their subordination was not only acceptable but necessary and good.

In his work *Politics*, Aristotle states clearly: "The male is by nature superior, and the female inferior; and the one rules, and the other is ruled; this principle, of necessity, extends to all mankind".

This was not casual observation—it was systematic philosophy. Aristotle grouped household relations into three categories of rule: master over slave, father over child, and husband over wife. Each relationship involved someone with reason ruling over someone with less reason. His assessment of women's rational capacity? "The slave is wholly lacking the deliberative element; the female has it but it lacks authority; the child has it but it is incomplete".

Let that sink in. According to Aristotle, women have the capacity for rational thought, but it "lacks authority"—meaning women can reason, but their reasoning should not be trusted or acted upon. They possess rationality but are naturally unfit to exercise it in any authoritative capacity. This conveniently justified excluding women from citizenship, which required rational deliberation about public affairs, while still allowing them to manage households and raise children.

But Aristotle went further. He described women as incomplete or "mutilated" males. "A female is an incomplete male or 'as it were, a deformity'". His biological theory held that in reproduction, the male actively provided form and soul through semen, while the female passively provided only matter. The male was the complete human; the female was what happened when development went wrong.

> ***Evidence for the Prosecution***: *The philosopher who shaped Western logic, ethics, and political theory for two millennia taught that women were essentially defective men, naturally suited to be ruled, rationally incomplete, and properly subordinate. His influence cannot be overstated—medieval scholastics, Enlightenment thinkers, and modern philosophers all built on Aristotelian foundations. His views on women were cited as authoritative truth for centuries.*

Modern scholars label Aristotle's views as "misogynistic" and note they "justified women's inferiority, influencing medieval and modern gender debates." One scholar notes that during the Middle Ages, "Aristotle's name was invoked by nearly every medieval misogynist writer, granting classical authority to anti-women rhetoric".

The Masculine Triad in Action:

• ***God/Philosophy***: *Aristotelian philosophy provided intellectual justification for female subordination, framing it as natural law*

• ***Man***: *Used this philosophy to exclude women from politics, education, and public life*

• ***Devil***: *Would later be associated with female intellect and independence which, Aristotelian thought had already deemed dangerous*

The Roman Republic: Freedom From Tyranny, Tyranny Over Women

Rome took the Greek model and refined it. The Roman Republic (509-27 BCE) was celebrated for overthrowing monarchy and establishing a government where power was distributed among citizens rather than concentrated in a king. Romans prized *libertas*—freedom from tyrannical rule—as their highest political value.

But Roman freedom, like Greek democracy, was exclusively male.

The Roman family was organized around the concept of *paterfamilias*—the male head of household who wielded absolute authority. The paterfamilias had power (*patria potestas*) over his wife, children, and slaves—power that included control over their persons, their property, and even their lives.

"This power meant originally not only that he had control over the persons of his children, amounting even to a right to inflict capital punishment, but that he alone had any rights in private law. Thus, acquisitions of a child became the property of the father". The same principle applied to wives. Everything a woman earned, inherited, or owned belonged legally to her husband or father.

Evidence for the Prosecution: Roman law gave men absolute power over the women in their households—the very definition of tyranny. Yet Romans never saw the contradiction between fighting for libertas in the public sphere while maintaining absolute male authority in the private sphere.

In early Roman marriage (*manus* marriage), "a bride passed from her father's control into the 'hand' (manus) of her husband. She then became subject to her husband's potestas"—literally, she was property transferred from one man to another. Though this form of marriage evolved into "free marriage" by the late Republic, even then, "the husband had the right to make the final decisions in all questions concerning the family".

Women could not vote, could not hold political office, and were "perpetually under the guardianship of a man, be it a father, husband, or other male relative". The legal principle was explicit: women could not be guardians themselves "propter sexus infirmitatem" (due to the weakness of their sex).

The paterfamilias had extraordinary powers:

- The right to kill his children of any age (*ius vitae necisque*)

- The right to decide whether a newborn would be allowed to live or would be exposed to die

- The right to sell his children into slavery

- Absolute ownership of all family property

Note that these powers did not extend equally to mothers. If a woman's husband died, his father (the grandfather) could take her children from her. "Women were often discouraged from divorcing their husbands because any children were the property of the paterfamilias. He had the right to refuse her any further contact with her children after a divorce".

*Evidence for the Prosecution: Roman law gave fathers
and husbands the power of life and death over women
and children. When men exercised such power in the
political sphere, Romans called it tyranny and fought*

*wars against it. When men exercised the same power in
the domestic sphere, Romans called it natural order and
enshrined it in law.*

The Founding Myth: Rape as Nation-Building

Perhaps no story better reveals Roman attitudes toward women than
the founding myth of Rome itself: the Rape of the Sabine Women.

According to legend, the first Romans were men without wives.
They invited the neighboring Sabine people to a festival, and during
the celebration, the Roman men abducted the Sabine women, taking
them by force to be their wives. When the Sabine men came to rescue
their daughters, the women—now pregnant or with Roman children—
intervened to stop the battle, choosing to remain with their Roman
husbands rather than return to their fathers.

This story, celebrated in Roman art and literature for centuries, is
presented not as a tale of horror but as the foundation of Roman
greatness. The abduction and rape of women is framed as necessary
nation-building. The women's eventual acceptance of their captors is
portrayed as their choice, not the result of having no other option.

Evidence for the Prosecution*: Rome's founding myth
glorifies the abduction and rape of women, framing male
violence against women as the heroic origin of
civilization. This is not an obscure legend—it was central
to Roman identity, depicted in countless artworks and
retold as a source of pride.*

The Exception That Proves the Rule: Spartan Women

We must briefly mention Sparta, because defenders of ancient Greece often point to Spartan women as evidence that Greek society could value female strength and autonomy.

It is true that Spartan women had more freedom than their Athenian counterparts. In Sparta, women could own property in their own right, and they participated in public exercise and athletic training. But this "freedom" existed for a specific reason: Spartan men were warriors, often away at war or living in military barracks. Women needed to be physically strong to manage estates and bear strong sons. Their relative autonomy served male military interests.

And even in Sparta, women could not vote, could not hold political office, and were still considered subordinate to male authority. Sparta granted women more physical freedom than Athens, but not political freedom, not equality, and not independence.

> ***Evidence for the Prosecution****: Even in the Greek city-state most celebrated for valuing strong women, that value was instrumental—women were valued for their utility in producing warriors, not as autonomous beings with rights to freedom and self-determination.*

The Great Contradiction: Liberty for Me, Subordination for Thee

Let us step back and examine the profound contradiction at the heart of Greek and Roman civilization:

These societies invented the language of citizenship, rights, and political participation. They developed sophisticated philosophical arguments about human nature, justice, and the good life. They fought wars against tyranny. They celebrated freedom as the highest political good. Their male citizens engaged in fierce debates about democracy versus oligarchy, about the rights of citizens versus the power of the state, about liberty and self-governance.

And throughout all of this, they never questioned—or actively defended—the complete subordination of half the human race.

When Pericles gave his famous Funeral Oration celebrating Athenian democracy, he spoke of citizens' equal rights and opportunities. He said nothing about the women present who had none of those rights. When Roman senators debated the nature of freedom, they did not see any contradiction in returning home to households where they held absolute power over wives and daughters. When Aristotle wrote about justice and the good life, he saw no injustice in declaring women naturally inferior.

> ***Evidence for the Prosecution****: The civilizations that gave the world democracy, republicanism, and political philosophy did so while systematically excluding women and providing elaborate intellectual justifications for that exclusion. The concepts of freedom and rights they developed applied only to men—and they knew it, and they defended it.*

This matters profoundly to our case. We often hear that women's subordination in ancient times was simply "the way things were," that everyone accepted it, that questioning it would have been unthinkable. But this is demonstrably false. The Greeks and Romans thought deeply about freedom, rights, justice, and tyranny. They debated these concepts endlessly. They just never extended the debate to include women—or when they did (as Plato tentatively did in *The Republic*), the suggestion was quickly dismissed or ignored.

They could have questioned female subordination. They chose not to. They could have extended citizenship to women. They chose not to. They could have applied their sophisticated theories of justice and rights to half the population. They chose not to.

Why? Because the Masculine Triad benefited from the arrangement. Men held all political power, all property rights, and all legal authority. Why would they voluntarily surrender that? Better to declare it "natural," to philosophize it into necessity, to enshrine it in law and custom so thoroughly that questioning it would seem absurd.

The Long Shadow

The exclusion of women from Athenian democracy and Roman republicanism was not merely ancient history. It became the foundation for Western political thought. When the American Founding Fathers studied ancient Greece and Rome as models for their new republic, they absorbed both the ideals of liberty *and* the exclusion of women. When Enlightenment philosophers wrote about natural rights, they built on Aristotelian foundations that defined women as naturally subordinate.

The intellectual architecture of Western civilization was constructed by men, for men, with women explicitly excluded from its definition of "human." And that architecture included elaborate philosophical justifications for why this exclusion was natural, necessary, and good.

Masculine Triad Actions in Greece and Rome:

- *__God/Religion__: While less prominent than in monotheistic societies, Greek and Roman religious practices still limited women (though they could be priestesses, their authority was constrained)*

- *__Man:__ Created political systems celebrating freedom while excluding women; developed legal systems giving men absolute power over women; produced philosophical justifications for female inferiority*

- *__Devil:__ Not a feature of Greek/Roman mythology in the same way, but female figures who transgressed boundaries (Medea, Clytemnestra) were portrayed as monstrous*

The Pattern Continues

We have now witnessed three stages of female subjugation:

- In Eden: theological foundation (woman created as subordinate, cursed for disobedience)

- In Mesopotamia: legal codification (women as property under written law)

- In Greece and Rome: philosophical justification (women as naturally inferior, democracy only for men)

Each stage built upon the previous. The theological subordination established in Genesis was enacted into Hammurabi's Code, which was then justified by Aristotelian philosophy, which in turn influenced

Roman law. By the time we reach the classical era, female subordination is justified by law, philosophy, and custom—a complete system with theological, intellectual, and legal support.

And the men who created this system? They called it civilization. They called it justice. They called it the natural order. They celebrated their freedom while denying it to women, and they never saw—or never admitted—the contradiction.

In Chapter 4, we turn to biblical law and early Christianity, where religious authority reinforced and intensified female subordination, giving divine sanction to the patterns established in earlier civilizations.

CHAPTER FOUR

Biblical Law and Early Christianity — Divine Mandate for Submission

When God commands obedience

We return now to religious authority, but with a crucial difference. In Chapter 1, we examined the Eden narrative—the mythological origin of female subordination. In this chapter, we examine how that origin story was translated into detailed legal codes, moral teachings, and ecclesiastical authority that governed women's lives for millennia.

If Eden established that women should be subordinate, the biblical legal tradition explained exactly how that subordination should work in practice. And when Christianity emerged from Judaism, it carried forward these restrictions while adding new dimensions of control—all with the authority of God Himself.

This chapter presents some of the most difficult evidence in our case, because it directly challenges religious texts that billions consider sacred. But our task is not to attack faith—it is to document how religious authority has been used to restrict female freedom. The evidence speaks for itself.

Old Testament Law: Regulating Female Bodies and Behavior

The Hebrew Bible contains extensive legal codes governing nearly every aspect of ancient Israelite life. Embedded within these codes are detailed regulations specific to women—regulations that controlled their sexuality, their purity, their economic value, and their legal status.

Women as Property in Marriage

The Ten Commandments, foundational to Judeo-Christian morality, include this instruction: "You shall not covet your neighbor's house; you shall not covet your neighbor's wife, or his male servant, or his female servant, or his ox, or his donkey, or anything that is your neighbor's" (Exodus 20:17).

Note the structure: wife is listed alongside house, servants, and livestock. She is property belonging to the husband, things that other men should not covet because they belong to someone else.

Marriage itself was a transaction between men. The groom paid a bride price to the father. Deuteronomy 22:28-29 states: "If a man meets a virgin who is not betrothed, and seizes her and lies with her, and they are found, then the man who lay with her shall give to the father of the young woman fifty shekels of silver, and she shall be his wife, because he has violated her. He may not divorce her all his days."

Evidence for the Prosecution*: Under biblical law, if a man raped an unmarried woman, the solution was financial compensation to her father and forced marriage to her rapist. The woman had no say. She was damaged property, and the solution was to force the man to purchase that damaged property and keep it permanently.*

Purity Laws: Control Through Contamination

Leviticus contains extensive laws regarding female "uncleanness"—menstruation, childbirth, and bodily functions. A menstruating woman was considered ritually impure for seven days, and anyone who touched her or anything she sat on also became impure (Leviticus 15:19-24). After giving birth, a woman was impure for 7 days after a male child, and 14 days after a female child—the message being clear that bearing a daughter was doubly polluting (Leviticus 12:1-5).

These purity laws had profound practical effects. Women could not participate in religious rituals during menstruation. They could not enter sacred spaces. They were isolated and marked as contaminating. The natural biological functions of the female body were framed as sources of impurity requiring purification.

> ***Evidence for the Prosecution****: God's law declared female biology itself as polluting. Women's normal bodily functions—menstruation and childbirth—rendered them ritually impure, requiring separation and cleansing. Male bodily functions received far less restrictive treatment.*

Sexual Control and Violent Enforcement

Biblical law enforced female chastity with brutal efficiency:

Deuteronomy 22:13-21 establishes that if a man married a woman and then claimed she was not a virgin, her parents must produce evidence of her virginity (the "tokens of virginity"—presumably bloodstained bedsheets). If they could not, "then they shall bring out the young woman to the door of her father's house, and the men of her city shall stone her to death with stones, because she has done an outrageous thing in Israel by whoring in her father's house."

Death by stoning. For premarital sex. For the woman.

What if the man's accusation was false? Deuteronomy 22:18-19: "The elders of that city shall take the man and whip him, and they shall fine him a hundred shekels of silver... he may not divorce her all his days." A whipping and a fine. She can be executed; he receives corporal punishment and a financial penalty.

> **Evidence for the Prosecution:** *Biblical law punished female sexual activity far more severely than male sexual activity. A woman could be stoned to death for not being a virgin on her wedding night. The double standard is embedded in divine law.*

Women as War Spoils

Numbers 31 recounts the war against the Midianites. After the battle, Moses was angry that the soldiers had spared the women and children. His command: "Now therefore, kill every male among the little ones, and kill every woman who has known man by lying with him. But all the young girls who have not known man by lying with him, keep alive for yourselves" (Numbers 31:17-18).

Virgin girls were war spoils—property to be distributed among the conquerors. The text goes on to detail how the spoils (including the virgin girls) were divided, with some going to the soldiers and some going to the Levites as offerings to the Lord.

> **Evidence for the Prosecution:** *Under biblical law, virgin women captured in war became property of the victors. God's command, delivered through Moses, explicitly*

ordered that virgin girls be kept alive "for yourselves"—a euphemism for sexual slavery.

New Testament: Continued Subordination in Christian Dress

When Jesus Christ emerged in the first century, some have argued he represented a more egalitarian approach to women. He spoke with women, taught women, and included women among his followers—actions that challenged some cultural norms of his time. Women were present at the crucifixion when male disciples fled, and women were the first witnesses to the resurrection.

But the Christian church that developed after Jesus's death quickly reverted to patterns of female subordination, now framed as Christian doctrine and apostolic teaching.

Paul's Instructions: Submission and Silence

The Apostle Paul, whose letters form much of the New Testament and shaped Christian theology for centuries, was explicit about female subordination:

"Wives, submit to your own husbands, as to the Lord. For the husband is the head of the wife even as Christ is the head of the church, his body, and is himself its Savior. Now as the church submits to Christ, so also wives should submit in everything to their husbands" (Ephesians 5:22-24).

This was not advice. This was apostolic command, presented as God's order for Christian marriage. The wife must submit "in everything"—a totalizing demand for obedience. The comparison to Christ and the church elevates male authority to divine parallel.

Even more restrictive: "Let a woman learn quietly with all submissiveness. I do not permit a woman to teach or to exercise authority over a man; rather, she is to remain quiet" (1 Timothy 2:11-12).

> ***Evidence for the Prosecution***: *Christian scripture explicitly forbids women from teaching or having authority over men. Women are commanded to silence and submissiveness. This was not cultural context or personal opinion—Paul presented it as divine instruction.*

Why must women be silent and subordinate? Paul provides biblical justification: "For Adam was formed first, then Eve; and Adam was not deceived, but the woman was deceived and became a transgressor" (1 Timothy 2:13-14).

The logic is clear: Because Eve was created second and was the one deceived in Eden, all women for all time must be subordinate and silent. Female subordination is justified by reference to the very origin story we examined in Chapter 1. The pattern repeats: Genesis establishes hierarchy, and subsequent teaching reinforces it.

Paul continues: "Let your women keep silent in the churches, for they are not permitted to speak; but they are to be submissive, as the law also says" (1 Corinthians 14:34).

Women could not speak in church. They could not teach. They could not lead. They were to be quiet, submissive, and subordinate—because "the law also says" so. Divine authority stacked upon divine authority, ensuring no escape.

Masculine Triad in Action:

• **God**: *Divine commands for female submission delivered through apostolic teaching*

• **Man**: *Male church leaders interpreting and enforcing these commands*

• **Devil**: *Eve's deception by the serpent used as eternal justification for silencing all women*

The Church Fathers: Amplifying the Subordination

As Christianity spread and developed institutional structure, the men who shaped church doctrine—the Church Fathers—took biblical teachings on female subordination and intensified them.

Tertullian (c. 155-240 CE) addressed women directly in his work *On the Apparel of Women*:

"Do you not know that you are each an Eve? The sentence of God on this sex of yours lives in this age: the guilt must of necessity live too. You are the devil's gateway: you are the unsealer of that forbidden tree: you are the first deserter of the divine law: you are she who persuaded him whom the devil was not valiant enough to attack. You destroyed so easily God's image, man. On account of your desert—that is, death—even the Son of God had to die."

> *Evidence for the Prosecution: One of the most influential early Christian writers called women "the devil's gateway" and blamed all women for the fall of humanity and the necessity of Christ's death. Every woman was collectively guilty of Eve's sin, forever.*

Augustine (354-430 CE), perhaps the most influential theologian in Christian history, developed the doctrine of original sin—the teaching that Adam's sin in Eden was transmitted to all humanity. But Augustine's formulation specifically blamed Eve and connected sin's transmission to the sexual act of procreation. Original sin passed through women's bodies in the act of reproduction. Every baby born was born sinful because of what Eve did and how sin was transmitted through female sexuality.

> *Evidence for the Prosecution: Augustine's theology of original sin made women's bodies the vehicle for transmitting spiritual corruption to all humanity. Sex became inherently sinful (even within marriage, according to some readings), and women bore special guilt as daughters of Eve.*

John Chrysostom (c. 347-407 CE), Archbishop of Constantinople, wrote: "The woman taught once, and ruined all. On this account... let her not teach. But what is it to other women, that she suffered this? It certainly concerns them; for the sex is weak and fickle."

Note his logic: Because Eve made a mistake, all women are unreliable and should never teach. An entire sex is condemned as "weak and fickle" based on one story from Genesis.

These were not fringe figures. These were the men who shaped Christian doctrine, whose writings were (and are) taught in seminaries, whose teachings influenced centuries of Christian practice and law. Their views on women became official church teaching, cited as authoritative truth.

> ***Evidence for the Prosecution****: The foundational teachers of Christianity taught that women were collectively guilty of humanity's fall, were the devil's gateway, were weak and fickle by nature, and were vehicles for transmitting sin. These teachings had divine authority and shaped how women were treated for centuries.*

The Practical Effects: Lived Subordination

These teachings were not mere theology—they had profound practical effects on women's lives.

Women could not be priests or hold ecclesiastical authority. The church, which increasingly controlled education, largely excluded women from formal learning. The same Tertullian who called women "the devil's gateway" also wrote extensively against women adorning themselves, wearing jewelry, or drawing attention—efforts to control female bodies and behavior through moral teaching.

Christian marriage, influenced by Paul's teachings, was explicitly hierarchical. The husband was the head, the wife must submit. Canon law (church law) governed marriage throughout medieval Europe, and it incorporated these biblical teachings. A woman's duty was submission; a man's was leadership. This wasn't negotiable—it was divine order.

When women did rise to positions of influence (as mystics, abbesses, or saints), their authority was always qualified, always exceptional, always requiring special justification. The default remained: women should be quiet, subordinate, and subject to male authority.

Masculine Triad Actions in Biblical Law and Early Christianity:

• *God*: *Extensive legal codes regulating female behavior, sexuality, and status; divine commands for submission; punishment systems targeting women more harshly*

• *Man*: *Male religious leaders interpreting scripture; male priests exercising ecclesiastical authority; male heads of household enforcing "biblical" marriage*

• *Devil*: *Blamed for Eve's fall, but this blame then used to justify subordinating all women; female sexuality and independence associated with demonic influence*

The Theological Trap

Let us identify the elegant trap that biblical law and Christian teaching created:

1. God created woman as subordinate (Genesis)

2. Woman's sin in Eden justified subordination as punishment (Genesis 3)

3. Old Testament law codified exactly how women should be controlled (Leviticus, Deuteronomy, etc.)

4. Jesus's teachings did not explicitly overturn these laws

5. Paul's letters reinforced female subordination as Christian doctrine

6. Church Fathers amplified these teachings, making female subordination essential to orthodoxy

7. Anyone who questioned female subordination was questioning God's word and apostolic teaching—was questioning divine authority itself

This is the perfect trap. A woman who desired freedom was not just going against custom or law—she was going against God. She was rebelling against divine order. She was repeating Eve's sin of desiring to be "like God." She was, in the words of the church, inspired by the Devil.

> ***Evidence for the Prosecution***: *Biblical law and Christian teaching created a theological system that made female subordination a matter of divine command, immune from questioning because questioning it meant questioning God Himself. Women were trapped by scripture, by theology, and by the authority of men who claimed to speak for God.*

The Counter-Evidence That Never Mattered

We should note, for intellectual honesty, that the Bible contains examples of women in leadership: Deborah the judge, Esther the queen, Huldah the prophetess, Mary Magdalene as witness to the resurrection, Phoebe as deaconess. Proverbs 31 praises the capable wife who engages in business and provides for her household.

But these examples were always treated as exceptions, not models. They were explained away or minimized. When women cited these examples to argue for expanded roles, they were told that these were special cases, that times had changed, that the general rule still applied.

The restrictive verses—the commands for silence, submission, and subordination—these were treated as universal and timeless. The examples of female leadership were treated as contextual and temporary. The asymmetry is telling.

***Evidence for the Prosecution**: When scripture presented women in positive or leadership roles, religious authorities treated these as exceptions. When scripture commanded female subordination, authorities treated these as universal law. The interpretation served to maintain male control.*

The Foundation Is Complete

We have now completed our examination of how female subordination was established across four chapters:

1. **Eden**: Theological foundation—woman created as helper, cursed with subordination

2. **Mesopotamia**: Legal codification—women as property under written law

3. **Greece and Rome**: Philosophical justification—women as naturally inferior

4. **Biblical Law**: Divine command—detailed regulations with God's authority

By the end of the ancient world, female subordination was supported by:

- Religious texts (Genesis, Leviticus, Deuteronomy, Pauline epistles)
- Philosophical systems (Aristotle and Greek thought)
- Legal codes (Hammurabi, Roman law, biblical law)
- Institutional authority (Church teaching and canon law)

This foundation was comprehensive and interlocking. Question one part, and defenders pointed to the others. Reject biblical teaching? They cited Aristotle. Reject Aristotle? They cited Genesis. Reject both? They pointed to centuries of law and custom, all claiming to reflect natural order and divine will.

The Masculine Triad had created a system where female subordination was simultaneously natural, divinely ordained, philosophically justified, and legally enforced.

As we move into Part II, we will see this foundation put to horrifying use. In the medieval period, the Masculine Triad's system of female control would reach its darkest expression: the systematic murder of women accused of witchcraft, thousands burned at the stake for the crime of being female and independent.

The foundation is laid. Now we see it in action.

• • •

PART II: THE MEDIEVAL TRIAD

CHAPTER FIVE

Medieval Europe — Property and Piety

The medieval period in Europe—roughly from 500 to 1500 CE—represents the Masculine Triad operating at peak efficiency. During these thousand years, the three arms of subordination—religious authority, demonic evil working through earthly systems, and patriarchal family control—worked in perfect coordination to create a comprehensive system where women existed as legal non-entities, theological inferiors, and family property. What had been established in ancient law and biblical doctrine now became woven into every fiber of European society.

Medieval Europe perfected the machinery of female subordination. Where ancient civilizations had subordinated women through specific laws or religious practices, medieval Europe created a totalizing system where women's legal, economic, social, and spiritual existence was entirely subsumed into male authority. A woman in medieval Europe literally did not exist as an independent person. She was her father's property until marriage, then became her husband's property, absorbed so completely into his legal identity that she ceased to exist as a separate entity in the eyes of law, church, and society.

Consider this: a married woman could not own the clothes on her back. She could not earn a wage in her own name. She could not enter a contract to buy bread. She could not write a will to leave her possessions to her children. She could not refuse her husband's sexual demands. She could not protect herself from his violence. She could not leave him no matter how brutal he became. And all of this—all of it—was not merely social custom. It was law, backed by religious doctrine, enforced by devilish systems of oppression, and replicated in every household.

Let us examine how each member of the Masculine Triad contributed to this comprehensive subjugation.

• • •

A Note on THE DEVIL

In Part I, we encountered THE DEVIL as a theological figure—the serpent in Eden, the tempter, the rebel angel. But THE DEVIL's role in the Masculine Triad extends beyond mythology. Throughout Parts II, III, and IV, THE DEVIL manifests as institutional power: the legal systems, courts, governments, and bureaucracies that transform ideology into enforceable reality. THE DEVIL is not merely supernatural evil; it is the machinery of the state that writes subordination into law and punishment into practice. The same force that tempted Eve in Eden now writes the laws that burn witches and deny women property rights. The form changes; the function remains.

Evidence for the Prosecution: GOD

The medieval Church stood as the dominant religious, intellectual, and often political force in European life. The Church owned approximately one-third of all land in Western Europe. It controlled education—universities were Church institutions, and literacy was almost entirely confined to the clergy. It regulated marriage, sexuality, and family life. It claimed authority over kings and emperors. And at every level, from papal pronouncements to village sermons, it taught that female subordination was God's will.

Where the early Church Fathers like Augustine and Jerome had articulated theological justifications for female subordination, medieval theologians systematized and elaborated these arguments into comprehensive philosophical frameworks that would dominate Western thought for centuries. These weren't abstract theological musings—they were the intellectual infrastructure that supported legal, political, and social oppression of women.

Thomas Aquinas and the "Misbegotten Male"

Thomas Aquinas (1225-1274), perhaps the most influential theologian in Christian history, synthesized Aristotelian philosophy with Christian doctrine to create what became the definitive medieval position on women. His *Summa Theologica* was not merely academic speculation—it shaped Church doctrine, university teaching, and legal reasoning across Europe for centuries. When popes needed theological justification for policy, they turned to Aquinas. When universities taught theology and philosophy, they taught Aquinas. When lawyers and judges needed to understand the natural order that law should reflect, they consulted Aquinas.

In Question 92 of the *Summa Theologica*, Aquinas addresses whether woman should have been made in the first production of things —whether, that is, God should have created women at all. His answer, drawing heavily from Aristotle, declares:

"As regards the individual nature, woman is defective and misbegotten, for the active force in the male seed tends to the production of a perfect likeness in the masculine sex; while the production of woman comes from defect in the active force or from some material indisposition, or even from some external influence; such as that of a south wind, which is moist."

Read that again slowly. According to the most respected theologian of the medieval period—a man whose works were placed beside the Bible itself by some popes—woman is *defective and misbegotten*. Her very existence represents a failure in the reproductive process. The natural aim of generation is to produce a male; a female is produced only when something goes wrong—a defect in the "active force," poor maternal material, or even the wrong direction of the wind.

Think about what this means. Every woman walking the earth is, according to official Church theology, a mistake. An error. A defect that shouldn't have happened. She exists because something went wrong during conception—because her father's seed was too weak, or her mother's womb was too poor, or the weather was bad that day.

This wasn't fringe theology or the opinion of one eccentric monk. This was mainstream Christian doctrine taught in every university, preached from every pulpit, cited in every legal and philosophical treatise. Aquinas's influence was so profound that Pope Leo XIII declared in 1879—more than 600 years after Aquinas's death—that Aquinas's theology was *the* exposition of Catholic doctrine and should be taught in all Catholic schools. At the Second Vatican Council in 1965, the Church reaffirmed that priests' theological education should be based on Aquinas's teachings.

His characterization of women as defective males shaped how the Church, the state, and society viewed female nature for centuries. It provided intellectual justification for denying women education (why waste resources educating defective beings?), excluding them from political power (defective beings shouldn't rule), and subordinating them in marriage (the defective must submit to the perfect).

Aquinas continues by arguing that woman exists solely for procreation. In addressing whether woman was necessary in the first creation, he states that for any purpose other than generation, "man can be more efficiently helped by another man than by woman." Woman's only function, her sole justification for existence, is to serve as a vessel for producing male heirs. She has no other value, no other purpose. A man needing help with work, counsel, companionship, intellectual discussion—for all these things, another man would be superior. Woman exists only to breed.

Moreover, Aquinas argues that female subjection existed even before the Fall—it is natural, not a punishment for sin. Eve's subordination to Adam wasn't a consequence of eating the forbidden fruit; it was built into creation itself. Women are inferior intellectually and morally:

"Woman is naturally subject to man, because in man the discretion of reason predominates."

Women lack the rational capacity for leadership, teaching, or authority. They are, by nature, ruled rather than ruling. Aquinas compares women's lack of wisdom to that of children and the insane— all categories of people who cannot be trusted with authority or responsibility because they lack proper use of reason.

This divine order—established at creation, confirmed by Scripture, elaborated by theology—demanded female submission as a matter of cosmic necessity. To resist male authority was to resist God's design for the universe. A woman who claimed equality with men wasn't just breaking social custom; she was defying the fundamental structure of reality as God had created it.

The Church's Control of Marriage

During the medieval period, marriage became a sacrament under exclusive Church control. This development, which occurred around the 12th century, gave the Church direct power over the most intimate and consequential decision in most women's lives. The Church determined who could marry whom, under what conditions, and with what consequences.

Theoretically, the Church required consent from both parties for a valid marriage. This sounds progressive until we understand the reality on the ground. A woman without economic resources, legal rights, or social standing had little practical ability to refuse a marriage her family arranged. If she refused, she faced being cut off from family support, losing any claim to inheritance, and being labeled as disobedient and unmarriageable. Moreover, the Church's definition of "consent" was minimal—simply not actively protesting could be construed as consent.

More importantly, Church law reinforced the subordination within marriage. A wife owed her husband the "conjugal debt"—the obligation to provide sexual access on demand. This wasn't mere theological opinion; Church courts would actually enforce a husband's right to his wife's body. Canon law explicitly stated that neither spouse could refuse the other, but in practice, this meant wives could not refuse husbands. A man who forced his wife sexually was not committing any sin or crime; he was claiming what was rightfully his.

Consider what this meant in practice. A woman in a medieval marriage could not control whether she became pregnant. She could not refuse sex even when she was exhausted from childcare, sick, or recovering from previous childbirth. She could not say no when pregnancy might kill her—and pregnancy often did kill women, as we shall see. Her body literally belonged to her husband, and the Church backed his ownership with divine authority.

Divorce was nearly impossible to obtain. The Church taught that marriage was indissoluble—what God had joined together, no man could put asunder. Annulments could occasionally be secured, but they required proof that the marriage had been invalid from the start (perhaps due to too-close blood relationship or previous marriage), and they were expensive, difficult to obtain, and typically available only to the wealthy and well-connected.

When marriages were annulled, women typically lost everything. They had no right to marital property—it all belonged to the husband. They had no custody of children, who legally belonged to the father. They had no right to support or maintenance. An annulment could leave a woman destitute and cut off from her own children overnight.

The Church's control of marriage thus trapped women in relationships regardless of abuse, incompatibility, or danger. A woman married to a violent drunkard who beat her daily and squandered all resources had no escape. The Church would counsel her to be more submissive, to suffer patiently as Christ suffered, to win her husband through gentle feminine behavior. It would not grant her divorce. It would not protect her from his violence. It would simply tell her that her suffering was God's will.

Spiritual Authority as Male Monopoly

Women were completely and permanently excluded from religious authority. They could not be priests, could not administer sacraments, could not preach, could not teach in mixed company. The clergy was entirely male, from the parish priest to the Pope. This exclusion was absolute and universal across Christian Europe.

Women could enter religious life as nuns, but even convents were subject to male oversight. Bishops and priests controlled the spiritual and often temporal affairs of women's religious houses. Nuns could not hear confessions, could not say Mass, could not administer the Eucharist. For these essential spiritual functions, they depended on male priests. Even women who had renounced the world and dedicated themselves entirely to God remained under male authority.

The theological justification for this exclusion was clear: women were unsuited for spiritual leadership because they were intellectually and morally inferior, because Eve had brought sin into the world, because Christ had chosen only male apostles, because Paul had commanded women to be silent in churches. Every possible theological argument was marshaled to ensure that women could never interpret Scripture, never shape doctrine, never exercise spiritual authority.

This exclusion from religious authority meant women had no voice in interpreting Scripture, no role in developing theology, no power to shape the doctrines that governed their lives. The men who controlled the Church created and enforced the theological justifications for women's subordination, and women had no institutional power to challenge these teachings. When women were told they must submit, they were told this was God's design—and the men who claimed to speak for God ensured there was no divine appeal, no possibility that God might say something different through women's voices.

The few women who did claim direct spiritual authority—mystics like Hildegard of Bingen or Julian of Norwich—had to couch their visions in language of submission and humility, emphasizing their own unworthiness and the extraordinary nature of God speaking through such unworthy vessels. They could claim God had chosen to speak through them despite their female inadequacy, but they could not claim that women in general had spiritual authority or insight equal to men.

The medieval Church thus fulfilled GOD's role in the Masculine Triad by providing comprehensive theological justification for female subordination (women as defective, inferior, and created solely for male use), controlling the institution of marriage that governed women's lives (trapping them in relationships and granting husbands sexual and physical power over them), and monopolizing spiritual authority so that divine will could only be interpreted by men (ensuring that God always spoke with a male voice supporting male power).

When women were told they must submit, they were told this was God's unchangeable design for the universe. And the men who claimed to speak for God made absolutely certain there was no possibility of appeal to a different divine authority.

• • •

Evidence for the Prosecution: THE DEVIL

If God provided the theological justification for female subordination, the Devil provided the earthly mechanisms of enforcement. Medieval legal and political systems operated with such systematic cruelty, such comprehensive oppression, such perfectly coordinated machinery of subjugation that we can only understand them as demonic. The Devil's work in medieval Europe was not dramatic possession or spectacular evil—it was the quiet, legal, systematic erasure of women from existence itself.

The Devil operates through systems that appear rational, legitimate, even divinely ordained. Medieval law was presented as natural order, as common sense, as the foundation of civilization. But strip away the pretense, and we see the Devil's handiwork: laws designed to ensure that half the population existed in legal slavery, economic dependence, and physical vulnerability.

Coverture: The Devil's Legal Erasure of Women

The doctrine of coverture emerged during the High Middle Ages (roughly the 12th and 13th centuries) and represents one of the Devil's most elegant achievements in legal oppression. Under coverture, a married woman's legal identity was completely absorbed into her husband's. The great legal scholar William Blackstone would later summarize the principle in his *Commentaries on the Laws of England* (1765), but he was describing a legal doctrine that had been firmly established in medieval England:

> *"By marriage, the husband and wife are one person in law: that is, the very being or legal existence of the woman is suspended during the marriage, or at least is incorporated and consolidated into that of the husband: under whose wing, protection, and cover, she performs every thing."*

The very being or legal existence of the woman is suspended during the marriage. This is not metaphor or exaggeration. This was the actual legal status of married women for most of European history. Upon marriage, a woman ceased to exist as a legal person. This is the Devil's work—the complete annihilation of a human being's legal existence while leaving her body alive to serve and suffer.

The legal term for a married woman was *feme covert*—literally, "covered woman." She was covered by her husband's legal identity. She disappeared under his legal personhood. Everything she was, everything she owned, everything she earned became his. The Devil had convinced society that this erasure was protection, that this annihilation was care, that this slavery was love.

What did this mean in practice? Let us be specific, because the horror is in the details:

• A *feme covert* could not own property in her own name. Any property she brought to marriage immediately became her husband's. If her father died and left her an inheritance, it became her husband's. If someone gave her a gift, it became her husband's. The clothes on her back belonged to her husband. She was a ghost who could possess nothing because she legally did not exist.

• A *feme covert* could not control her own earnings. If she worked— and many women did work, in fields, in family businesses, in textile production, as servants—her wages legally belonged to her husband. He could collect them and spend them as he wished. She had no right to any portion of money she earned through her own labor. She could work herself to exhaustion and starve while her husband spent her wages on drink. This was legal. This was the Devil's economy.

• A *feme covert* could not enter into contracts. She could not buy or sell goods legally. She could not lease property. She could not run a business in her own name. Any contract she attempted to make was void. She was a legal phantom who could not engage in the economic transactions necessary for survival.

• A *feme covert* could not sue or be sued in her own name. If someone harmed her, stole from her, or broke a contract with her, she had no legal standing to seek remedy. If she harmed someone else, her husband was legally responsible. She had no legal agency, no access to justice, no recourse when wronged.

• A *feme covert* could not make a will without her husband's permission. She had no power to determine what would happen to her possessions (though they were actually his possessions) after her death. She could not even control the distribution of property after her own death.

• A *feme covert*'s body was not her own. Rape within marriage was not recognized as a crime because a husband had legal rights to sexual access to his wife. The concept of "marital rape" would not be recognized in English law until the 1990s—yes, the 1990s. The principle of coverture gave husbands ownership of their wives' bodies. The Devil had written into law that a woman's body was property to be used at will.

Even her children belonged legally to her husband. Upon his death, he could appoint a guardian for the children, and the mother—their actual mother who had given birth to them and cared for them—had no legal right to challenge this appointment. If a marriage ended (which was rare, as we've seen), the husband retained custody. The mother had no parental rights whatsoever. She was not legally recognized as having any relationship to her own children. The Devil had severed even the bond between mother and child.

Consider the totality of this legal erasure. A woman could work every day, earning wages through her labor, and have no legal right to a single penny she earned. She could inherit a fortune from her parents, and all of it would instantly become her husband's with no compensation to her. She could be beaten, raped, robbed by her husband, and the law provided her no remedy because legally she and he were the same person, and a person cannot steal from himself or assault himself.

This was the Devil's masterwork: a legal system so comprehensive in its oppression that it erased women from existence while keeping them alive to serve, work, and suffer.

Unmarried women—*feme sole*, or "women alone"—had somewhat more legal capacity. They could own property, make contracts, and sue in their own names. But society pressured women intensely to marry. An unmarried woman faced limited economic opportunities (most lucrative trades excluded women), social stigma (she was pitied, mocked, or suspected of sexual impropriety), and economic insecurity (without a husband's income, how would she live?).

For most women, marriage was economically necessary for survival, which meant surrendering all legal existence. The "choice" to marry was like the "choice" between surrendering your legal personhood or starving in the streets. The Devil had ensured that both paths led to suffering—one through legal erasure, the other through poverty and social death.

The Devil's Feudal Hierarchy: Exclusion from Power

The feudal system was built on land tenure and military service. Lords granted land (fiefs) to vassals in exchange for military service and political loyalty. These relationships created the political and military structure of medieval society. The Devil ensured that women were almost entirely excluded from this system because they were excluded from the activities that created feudal bonds: military service and the oath of fealty.

Women could not typically become vassals, could not swear fealty, could not owe military service. The feudal contract was between men. Even when noblewomen inherited land (which typically only happened in the absence of male heirs), their political rights were severely constrained. A woman who held land in her own right was expected to have a male guardian or marry quickly so that a man could exercise the political and military obligations that came with landholding.

This was not accident or oversight. The Devil had designed a system where power flowed only through male channels. Political authority, military might, economic control—all required participation in the feudal hierarchy, and the feudal hierarchy was closed to women.

Queens and noblewomen might exercise power as regents for underage sons or in the absence of husbands, but this was understood as temporary stewardship, not legitimate authority in their own right. And even royal women with vast landholdings operated within a system designed by and for men—a system designed by the Devil to ensure that power never truly rested in female hands.

Eleanor of Aquitaine is often cited as an example of female power in the Middle Ages—she was duchess in her own right, queen consort of both France and England, politically active and influential. Yet even Eleanor spent sixteen years imprisoned by her husband Henry II when she supported their sons' rebellion against him. Royal blood, vast landholdings, and political acumen couldn't protect her from her husband's authority backed by law. When she acted independently in ways that threatened his power, he simply locked her up. And this was legal. This was his right as her husband.

The Devil had created a system where even the most powerful woman could be caged by an ordinary exercise of male authority. If Eleanor of Aquitaine—duchess, queen, mother of kings—could be imprisoned for sixteen years for daring to act politically, what hope did ordinary women have?

The Devil's Gift: Legal Violence Against Women

Medieval law gave husbands the explicit legal right to "chastise" or "correct" their wives through physical punishment. While some legal codes placed theoretical limits on this—a man shouldn't maim or kill his wife—enforcement was virtually nonexistent. The Devil had written into law that violence against women was not merely permitted but necessary for proper household management.

Domestic violence was considered a private matter between husband and wife, and courts were extremely reluctant to intervene. This wasn't neglect; it was policy. The Devil had ensured that the state would protect male violence by refusing to acknowledge it as a public concern.

The famous "rule of thumb"—that a man could beat his wife with a stick no thicker than his thumb—is likely apocryphal as a specific legal rule. But whether or not courts ever articulated this exact standard, the reality was clear: wife-beating was legal, socially acceptable, and religiously sanctioned. Conduct manuals and sermons told husbands they had a duty to discipline disobedient wives. Legal treatises confirmed husbands' right to use physical force to control their households.

A man who killed his wife might face prosecution for murder—though even here, if he could claim she provoked him or was disobedient, he might receive a lighter sentence. But a man who merely beat her, even severely, faced no legal consequences. The beating wasn't a crime. It was his right as her husband. The Devil had made violence not only legal but mandatory for maintaining proper order.

Women had virtually no legal recourse. They couldn't leave violent husbands (where would they go? with what resources?). They couldn't divorce them. They couldn't appeal to courts for protection (courts would tell them to be more obedient). The law that should have protected them instead gave their abusers legal authority to abuse them.

This is the Devil's genius: to create systems where victims have no recourse, where oppression is law, where cruelty is duty. The Devil doesn't need dramatic acts of evil when he can write oppression into the legal code and call it civilization.

THE DEVIL thus fulfilled his role in the Masculine Triad by creating legal structures that denied women independent existence (coverture), excluded them from political power (feudalism's male-only bonds), and granted husbands authority to control and punish wives (legal domestic violence). Through law, the Devil ensured that women had no standing, no rights, no property, no recourse, and no escape.

The machinery of oppression was presented as natural law, as social order, as the foundation of civilization. But strip away the pretense, and we see it for what it is: the Devil's systematic enslavement of half the human race, enforced by law, blessed by the Church, and replicated in every household in Christendom.

• • •

Evidence for the Prosecution: MAN

Within the medieval household, the father's authority was absolute, divinely ordained, and legally unchallengeable. The family was understood as a microcosm of the broader social order—as God ruled the universe and the king ruled the kingdom, the father ruled the family. This wasn't mere analogy. It was the fundamental organizing principle of society, and in the household, Man exercised direct, daily, physical control over women.

If God provided the theological justification and the Devil provided the legal mechanisms, Man provided the enforcement. Every day, in every home, fathers and husbands wielded the power that God blessed and the Devil legalized. Man was the visible face of the Triad, the immediate oppressor, the one whose hands struck and whose voice commanded.

Patriarchal Authority in the Household

Medieval conduct literature and household manuals make painfully clear the extent of male authority in the family. The husband was lord and master of his household. He controlled all property and resources. He made all decisions regarding the family's economic, social, and spiritual life. His wife and children owed him absolute obedience— not merely deference or respect, but absolute obedience as a servant owes a master.

A wife's primary duty was submission. Medieval marriage vows, derived from St. Paul's epistles, required wives to promise obedience. The husband promised to love and cherish; the wife promised to love, honor, and *obey*. This wasn't merely ceremonial language. It was a legally enforceable obligation. A disobedient wife could be physically punished, denied resources, and socially shamed—all with full legal and social approval.

Women's labor belonged to their husbands. Whether a woman worked in the household (cooking, cleaning, brewing, weaving, spinning, caring for children and elderly family members) or in a family business (helping in a shop, working in fields, producing goods for sale), the fruits of her labor belonged to her husband. She had no right to compensation, no claim to any portion of what she produced. Her labor was his property.

Consider the enormity of women's unpaid labor. A medieval housewife rose before dawn to start fires, carried water (often from a well some distance away), cooked all meals from scratch over an open fire, cleaned, laundered clothing (a physically brutal task involving harsh soaps and heavy wet fabric), tended animals, preserved food for winter, spun thread, wove cloth, sewed and mended all clothing, cared for children and sick family members, and more. This was backbreaking work, endless work, essential work—work without which the household could not function.

And she had no legal right to any compensation, any property earned through this labor, or any voice in how household resources were spent. A woman could work sixteen-hour days keeping her family alive and have no right to a scrap of bread unless her husband chose to give it to her. Man had claimed ownership not just of women's bodies but of their labor, their time, their very capacity to work.

Women as Economic Burdens and Breeding Stock

Daughters were economic burdens on medieval families. Because they could not inherit land (or inherited only in the absence of male heirs), because they could not continue the family name, because under coverture any property they brought to marriage would immediately belong to another man's family, daughters required dowries to secure marriages.

The dowry system meant that families essentially had to pay men to take their daughters. The size of the dowry often determined the quality of husband a family could secure—a large dowry might secure a wealthy or high-status husband; a small dowry meant a poor match or spinsterhood. Families with multiple daughters faced serious financial strain. Some families simply couldn't afford to marry off all their daughters and would send "excess" daughters to convents (which also required payment, though typically less than a marriage dowry).

Daughters had no say in these arrangements. Marriage was a financial transaction between her father and her prospective husband. She was the commodity being exchanged—her labor, her body, her reproductive capacity were what the husband was purchasing with his agreement to accept a dowry. Man sold his daughters to other men, and the transaction was called marriage.

Once married, a woman's value lay almost entirely in her reproductive capacity. She was expected to produce children, preferably male heirs. The primary purpose of marriage, according to Church teaching, was procreation. A wife who failed to conceive, who produced only daughters, who suffered repeated miscarriages, faced blame, social stigma, and sometimes abandonment.

Man demanded that women breed, and the breeding often killed them.

Childbirth in medieval Europe was extraordinarily dangerous. Recent scholarship suggests that while dramatic claims of "one in three women died in childbirth" are exaggerated, the lifetime risk was still significant. For married women who had multiple pregnancies, the cumulative risk meant that approximately one in eighteen married women died from childbirth or its complications—far higher than today's risk of one in 2,400 in modern Europe.

But the raw mortality statistics don't capture the full horror. Death in childbirth was often slow and agonizing. Obstructed labor could last for days, leaving women exhausted, in excruciating pain, sometimes dying slowly as their tissues tore and infection set in. Hemorrhage could leave women bleeding to death over hours while family members watched helplessly. Puerperal fever (childbed fever, caused by infection) could kill women days or weeks after delivery, often leaving them delirious with fever, knowing they were dying and would leave their newborn motherless.

Medieval medical knowledge could do little to help. Midwives had practical experience but limited ability to intervene in truly complicated births. Caesarean sections were performed only on dead or dying mothers in desperate attempts to save the baby—the mother's survival was not expected. Women approached childbirth with real terror, often writing their wills beforehand and saying goodbye to their other children in case they didn't survive.

Yet despite these very real dangers, women had no choice about whether to risk pregnancy. The conjugal debt meant they could not refuse sex. There were no effective means of contraception available to them (the Church forbade even the unreliable methods that existed). Women's bodies were breeding grounds whether or not pregnancy might kill them, whether or not they wanted more children, whether or not they had the health or resources to care for another child.

Man had decided that women existed to produce children, and women died by the thousands producing them. Their deaths were called God's will. Their suffering was called natural. Their lack of choice was called duty. But it was Man—individual men, fathers and husbands—who demanded the pregnancies that killed their wives and daughters.

Women were expected to continue bearing children until they couldn't anymore—until age, exhaustion, or death ended their fertility. A woman might have eight, ten, twelve pregnancies over her reproductive life. Each pregnancy risked her life. Each birth damaged her body further. And she had no power to stop this cycle. Man had turned women's bodies into factories for producing children, and the factories ran until they broke.

Widowhood: Limited Freedom Under Male Control

Widows occupied a peculiar position in medieval society. As *feme sole*, they had legal capacity—they could own property, make contracts, conduct business. But this independence was limited and often temporary.

A widow's rights to her deceased husband's property depended on complex customs and local laws. In England, the custom of *dower* typically gave a widow use of one-third of her husband's lands for her lifetime. But she didn't own this property outright—she merely had the right to use it and collect its income during her life. Upon her death, it reverted to her husband's heirs.

This meant a widow could never sell the land or leave it to her own children (if she had children from another marriage or wanted to leave it to daughters). She held it only for life, only at the sufferance of her husband's family, who might resent her claim to "their" inheritance and pressure her to give it up or remarry.

Moreover, widows faced intense pressure to remarry, especially if they were young and held significant property. A woman of childbearing age with land and resources was a valuable commodity. Man wanted control of that property, control of that reproductive capacity. Feudal lords could pressure widows on their estates to remarry—a widow holding land meant uncollected military service and rent that the lord wanted properly managed by a male vassal. Wealthy widows were sometimes coerced into marriages they didn't want because their consent was never truly free when the alternative was losing everything.

Even in widowhood—even after a woman had escaped one man through his death—other men worked to reclaim control over her. The brief window of freedom a widow might experience was always precarious, always threatened, always subject to male authority reasserting itself.

Older widows or those without significant property might remain unmarried, but they often lived in poverty. Without a husband's income and with limited economic opportunities for women, many widows struggled to survive. Elderly widows swelled the ranks of the poor, dependent on charity or family members who might or might not help them. Man had created an economic system where women could barely survive without male support, and widows paid the price.

Sexual Control and Violence

Medieval men exercised comprehensive control over women's sexuality. Before marriage, daughters were closely supervised to preserve their virginity—a woman's sexual purity directly affected her marriage value and family honor. Fathers and brothers policed young women's interactions with men, their movements outside the home, their behavior, even their clothing. A woman who lost her virginity before marriage was "damaged goods," unmarriageable or worth only a greatly reduced dowry.

Man guarded women's virginity not to protect women but to protect his own property interest. A daughter's virginity was valuable because it increased her bride price. Her sexuality belonged to her father until he sold it to her husband.

After marriage, husbands controlled wives' sexuality completely. A wife could not refuse her husband sexually—this was the conjugal debt, legally and religiously mandated. But adultery by a wife was a serious crime, punishable by severe penalties including public shaming, physical punishment, or death. Male adultery, by contrast, was generally tolerated. A husband who kept mistresses or visited prostitutes faced no legal consequences and minimal social disapproval.

The double standard was explicit and enforced: women's sexuality belonged exclusively to their husbands, but men faced few restrictions on their sexual behavior. Man had written the rules to serve himself—he could use his wife's body at will while denying her any sexual autonomy, and he could seek sexual pleasure elsewhere while violently punishing her for the same.

Sexual violence against women was widespread and rarely punished. Rape laws theoretically protected women, but prosecution was difficult and conviction rare. The woman's sexual history, reputation, behavior, and clothing would all be scrutinized. If she had any sexual experience, if she had any reputation for impropriety, if she had been in the wrong place or dressed the wrong way, the rape would be seen as partly or entirely her fault.

If a woman was raped by her husband, it wasn't legally rape at all. The concept of marital rape didn't exist. A husband forcing his wife sexually was simply exercising his marital rights. If she was raped by another man and became pregnant, some legal codes actually forced her to marry her rapist—rewarding him and permanently tying her to her abuser. Man had made rape invisible, unpunishable, sometimes even rewarded.

MAN thus fulfilled his role in the Masculine Triad by exercising absolute authority over women in his household (controlling all decisions and resources), controlling women's labor and reproduction (extracting unpaid labor and forcing continuous pregnancy), policing women's sexuality (enforcing virginity before marriage and fidelity after while facing no such restrictions himself), and using violence to enforce submission (with full legal and social approval).

In every medieval home, Man ruled with the blessing of God and the protection of the Devil's laws. Women had nowhere to turn, nowhere to run, no recourse, no escape. The Triad was complete.

• • •

The Perfected System

Medieval Europe represents the Masculine Triad at its most comprehensive and systematic. Unlike earlier periods where women might be subordinated in some spheres but retain limited agency in others, medieval Europe created a totalizing system where every avenue of independence was closed, every door to freedom was locked, every possibility of escape was eliminated.

Consider the situation of a medieval woman in its full totality:

God told her she was a defective being, created from man's rib as an afterthought, prone to sin and deception, intellectually and morally inferior, existing solely to serve male needs. The Church controlled marriage, ensuring she had no escape from an abusive or unwanted union, commanding her to submit sexually to her husband's demands, offering her no protection from violence and no possibility of divorce.

The Devil denied her legal existence upon marriage, making her unable to own property, control her earnings, make contracts, sue for justice, or protect her children. Demonic legal structures excluded her from political power and military obligation, ensuring she could never wield the authority that came from land ownership or martial prowess. The Devil's laws explicitly granted her husband the right to beat her, and she had no legal recourse, no protection, no escape.

Man—her father, her husband, her brothers, her sons—exercised absolute authority over her body, her labor, her movements, her reproduction, and her life. She worked endlessly without compensation or rest, her labor enriching her household while she had no claim to its products. She was forced into continuous pregnancy despite very real risks of death, and she had no power to refuse or control her fertility. Her children legally belonged to their father, not to her.

Where could such a woman turn?

If she appealed to religion, priests quoted Scripture and Aquinas on female inferiority and submission, telling her to accept her suffering as God's will.

If she sought legal remedy, courts told her she had no legal standing to bring suit, that her very existence was merged into her husband's.

If she tried to leave her husband, she had no resources, no legal rights to her children, no means of economic survival, and nowhere to go.

If she resisted her subordination, she faced violence backed by law, scorn backed by religion, and destitution backed by economic reality.

The three arms of the Triad reinforced each other perfectly. Each made the others stronger. Each closed off avenues of escape that might have remained open if only one or two arms were active. Together, they created an inescapable prison.

This wasn't accidental, wasn't the result of uncoordinated prejudices happening to align. The medieval period saw the systematic development and refinement of patriarchal control. Theologians elaborated philosophical justifications for female inferiority, creating frameworks that could answer any objection and defeat any claim to equality. The Devil's servants developed legal doctrines like coverture that formalized women's subordination with elegant comprehensiveness. Men created social customs and economic structures that made women absolutely dependent on male protection and provision.

The system was comprehensive, coordinated, and devastatingly effective. For a thousand years, it subordinated half the population so thoroughly that most women accepted their subordination as natural, inevitable, and divinely ordained. The machinery of oppression was so thorough that women internalized it, teaching their daughters to submit, preparing their sons to rule, and policing other women who stepped out of line.

Yet even this perfected machinery of subordination would prove insufficient when women stepped too far out of line. Even total legal erasure, theological justification, and economic dependence couldn't always control women completely. Some women still claimed independence, still possessed knowledge that gave them power, still refused to submit entirely to male authority.

Some women healed the sick with knowledge passed down through generations of women. Some women lived independently, supporting themselves through their own labor and skill. Some women were too old to bear children and thus no longer useful for Man's purposes. Some women simply refused to be broken, refused to submit, refused to accept that their defective nature meant they deserved subordination.

For these women—for women who existed outside male control, women who possessed healing knowledge, women who were too independent or too assertive or too knowledgeable or simply too old to be useful—the Masculine Triad would deploy its ultimate weapon.

When persuasion failed, when law wasn't enough, when even violence within the home couldn't break a woman's spirit, the system would turn to mass murder. The Triad would burn them. Not metaphorically. Literally. By the tens of thousands.

As we shall see in the next chapter, when the system felt threatened, when women claimed too much independence, too much knowledge, too much power, the Masculine Triad would unleash hell on earth.

The witch hunts were coming.

CHAPTER SIX

The Burning Times — Witch Hunts and Femicide

Between 1450 and 1750—three hundred years spanning the late medieval period and the early modern era—Europe experienced a systematic campaign of mass murder that targeted women. Historians estimate that between 40,000 and 100,000 people were executed for witchcraft during this period. Approximately 75-85% of those killed were women. This was not random violence. This was not mob hysteria spiraling out of control. This was the Masculine Triad deploying its ultimate weapon: state-sanctioned, religiously blessed, male-enacted femicide.

When the perfected system of medieval subordination proved insufficient—when women still claimed independence despite legal erasure, still possessed knowledge despite theological denunciation of their intellectual capacity, still exercised power despite economic dependence on men—the Triad turned to elimination. If women could not be controlled, they would be killed.

The witch hunts were not an aberration. They were the logical conclusion of centuries of escalating oppression. When God declared women defective, when the Devil erased them legally, when Man controlled them domestically, and *still* some women refused to submit —the Triad's response was fire.

• • •

Who Were the Witches?

Before we examine how the Masculine Triad orchestrated this genocide, we must understand who was targeted. The stereotype of the witch—the old hag stirring a cauldron, cackling over spells—obscures the reality. The witch hunts targeted specific categories of women, and the pattern reveals the system's true purpose: eliminating women who existed outside male control.

The Healers and Midwives

Women who possessed medical knowledge were prime targets. Midwives, herbalists, and healers—women who had knowledge passed down through generations of women, knowledge that made them valuable and powerful in their communities—were systematically accused of witchcraft.

Consider the brutal logic: A midwife attended every birth. She possessed knowledge of women's bodies, of herbs that could ease pain or prevent pregnancy, of techniques that could save a mother's or infant's life. She was called to the bedsides of the sick. She knew which plants could heal and which could harm. And she exercised this knowledge independently, outside the control of the male-dominated medical establishment and male-controlled Church.

This knowledge was intolerable to the Masculine Triad. The Church taught that pain in childbirth was God's punishment for Eve's sin—to relieve that pain was to interfere with divine judgment. Male physicians, trained in universities that excluded women, resented competition from female healers whose empirical knowledge often surpassed their own theoretical training. Husbands feared wives who knew how to prevent pregnancy or end it.

When a baby died in childbirth—a common occurrence given medieval medical limitations—who was blamed? Not God's will. Not natural causes. The midwife. She must have killed it. She must have offered it to the Devil. She must be a witch.

When a woman successfully relieved labor pains with belladonna or other herbs, she was accused of witchcraft. When she failed to save a mother or child despite her best efforts, she was accused of witchcraft. There was no winning. The knowledge itself was the crime. A woman who knew things, who could do things, who had power through her knowledge—this was intolerable.

The Independent Women

Women who lived independently—widows who didn't remarry, single women who supported themselves, women who owned property or ran businesses—were disproportionately accused. The logic is clear: these women existed outside the direct control of individual men. They had no husband to govern them, no father to command them. They were ungoverned women in a system built on the premise that all women must be governed.

Older women were particularly vulnerable. Past childbearing age, they were no longer useful for breeding. If widowed and childless, they had no male relatives obligated to support them. They might become burdens on their communities, dependent on charity. Or they might support themselves through skills—healing, midwifery, selling goods —which gave them a measure of independence and respect.

Either way, they were dangerous. Women past male sexual use, past breeding utility, claiming space and resources for themselves—the Triad had no category for such women except "witch."

The Women Who Refused to Submit

Women described as "quarrelsome," "difficult," "sharp-tongued," or "aggressive" were accused far more often than docile women. The crime wasn't witchcraft. The crime was refusing to be properly submissive. The crime was talking back, standing up for themselves, asserting their rights, challenging male authority.

A woman who argued with her husband in public. A woman who refused unreasonable demands. A woman who defended herself verbally against insults or accusations. A woman who simply wouldn't shut up and submit—she was a witch.

The witch hunts weren't about stopping supernatural evil. They were about terrorizing women into submission. Burn enough outspoken women, and the message becomes clear: silence is survival. Submission is safety. Challenge male authority and burn.

The Women Someone Wanted Gone

Many accused witches were simply women someone wanted to eliminate for entirely mundane reasons. A widow with property her late husband's relatives wanted. A woman who rejected a man's sexual advances. A woman who knew a secret someone needed buried. A wife a husband wanted rid of but couldn't divorce.

Witchcraft accusations were weapons. Once the machinery of persecution was running, anyone could level an accusation. The accused woman was presumed guilty—proving innocence was nearly impossible. Under torture, she would confess to anything. Then she would burn, and her accuser would get what he wanted: her property, his secret kept, his revenge, his inconvenient wife eliminated.

The witch hunts created a system where women could be legally murdered on the basis of accusation alone. This wasn't a bug in the system. It was a feature. The Masculine Triad had created the perfect mechanism for eliminating any woman, anywhere, anytime, for any reason.

• • •

Evidence for the Prosecution: GOD

The Church provided the theological framework that made witch hunts possible and righteous. Without the Church's blessing, without God's supposed authority behind the persecution, the witch hunts could not have achieved their scale or brutality.

The Theological Foundation: Women as Devil's Gateway

The Church had spent centuries teaching that women were spiritually inferior, morally weak, intellectually deficient, and prone to sin. Eve had brought evil into the world. Women's carnal nature made them susceptible to temptation. Their defective reason made them unable to resist the Devil.

All of this created the perfect foundation for witch hunting theology: If women are naturally prone to evil and weak against temptation, of course they would make pacts with Satan. If they are intellectually inferior and easily deceived, of course the Devil could trick them. If they are carnally insatiable, of course they would fornicate with demons.

The theology that had justified subordinating women for centuries now justified killing them. The progression was seamless: women are defective → women are prone to sin → women are susceptible to the Devil → women are witches → women must be destroyed.

The Malleus Maleficarum: God's Instruction Manual for Femicide

In 1486, a Dominican inquisitor named Heinrich Kramer published *Malleus Maleficarum*—"The Hammer of Witches." This book became the definitive guide for identifying, prosecuting, and executing witches. It would be reprinted dozens of times and used across Europe for over two centuries. It was, quite literally, an instruction manual for mass murder of women.

The *Malleus* opens with the question: "Why is it that women are chiefly addicted to evil superstitions?" Kramer's answer draws on centuries of Christian misogyny. Women are more credulous than men. They have "slippery tongues" and cannot keep secrets. They are "more carnal than a man." They were formed from a "bent rib" and thus are inherently "defective." Most damningly: "All witchcraft comes from carnal lust, which is in women insatiable."

The *Malleus* specifically targets midwives, declaring: "No one does more harm to the Catholic Faith than midwives." Why? Because midwives possessed knowledge of women's bodies, could prevent conception, could facilitate abortions, attended births without male supervision. Their knowledge was power, and their power was intolerable.

The book provided detailed instructions for identifying witches (any woman could be one), interrogating them (torture was recommended), obtaining confessions (torture made everyone confess), and executing them (burning was preferred). It taught that women who didn't cry during interrogation were definitely witches—they had been hardened by Satan. Women who did cry were probably faking to seem innocent—also witches.

There was no escape. The *Malleus* created an epistemological trap where any response proved guilt. Accused of witchcraft and you confess under torture? Guilty. Refuse to confess despite torture? Guilty—the Devil is protecting you. Survive the torture? Guilty—Satan gave you supernatural endurance. Die during torture? Guilty—Satan summoned you to hell rather than let you reveal the coven's secrets.

The Church claimed to speak for God. God spoke through the Church. And the Church, through the *Malleus* and countless sermons and theological treatises, declared: women are witches, witches must burn, and this burning is holy work.

Purging the World of Evil—Or Purging the World of Women?

The genius of the Church's witch hunting theology was that it made femicide holy. Burning women wasn't murder—it was saving souls. It wasn't cruelty—it was protecting Christian civilization from Satan's agents. It wasn't genocide—it was necessary purification.

Priests blessed the executions. Clergy supervised the trials. Religious authorities signed the death warrants. And throughout it all, they invoked God's name. God commanded it. God demanded it. God would judge them for the witches they failed to burn, not the innocents they mistakenly killed.

Better to burn a hundred innocent women than let one guilty witch live—this was the operating principle. And since any woman could be a witch, since female nature itself was suspect, the potential pool of victims was infinite.

The Church thus fulfilled GOD's role in the witch hunts by providing theological justification (women as defective and evil by nature), creating the definitive guide for persecution (the *Malleus Maleficarum*), and blessing the executions as holy work (making mass murder of women a sacred duty).

• • •

Evidence for the Prosecution: THE DEVIL

The Devil's role in the witch hunts was to transform theological justification into legal machinery. The Devil took the Church's teachings and wrote them into law, created court procedures that guaranteed conviction, and built a system of persecution that could operate efficiently across all of Europe.

The Legal Machinery of Mass Murder

The witch trials were legal proceedings. They had courts, judges, prosecutors, formal charges, interrogation procedures, standards of evidence. This wasn't mob violence—it was state-sanctioned execution carried out through official legal channels. This was the Devil's specialty: making evil appear lawful, making murder look like justice.

The legal procedures for witch trials were designed to guarantee conviction. Accusation was effectively proof of guilt—the burden was on the accused to prove innocence, which was nearly impossible.

Torture was standard procedure for extracting confessions. Under torture, people will confess to anything—flying on broomsticks, fornicating with demons, eating babies, attending witches' sabbaths. These confessions, obtained through agony, were accepted as legal proof.

Once a woman confessed (and under torture, she would), she might be offered mercy if she named others. So torture produced not just one victim but a cascade of accusations. Each tortured woman, desperate to make the pain stop, would name other women. Those women would be arrested, tortured, and forced to name more women. The persecution could spread exponentially.

Some regions developed terrible innovations in legal procedure. In parts of Germany, witch trials allowed accusers to remain anonymous— a woman might be burned without ever knowing who accused her or why. Some courts allowed "spectral evidence"—testimony that the accused's spirit or specter had appeared to someone in a dream. You could be convicted and executed based on someone's nightmare.

This was the Devil's legal genius: create procedures that appear legitimate while guaranteeing conviction. Make it look like justice while engineering mass murder.

The Witch-Finders: Professional Killers

As the witch hunts intensified, professional witch-finders emerged— men who traveled from town to town offering their services in identifying and prosecuting witches. They were paid per conviction, creating a direct financial incentive for finding as many witches as possible.

The most notorious was Matthew Hopkins, who called himself "Witchfinder General" in England during the 1640s. In just two years, Hopkins was responsible for the deaths of more women than had been executed for witchcraft in the previous century in England. His methods included sleep deprivation (keep the accused awake for days until she was delirious and would confess to anything), "swimming" (bind the accused and throw her in water—if she floats, she's a witch protected by Satan; if she sinks and drowns, she was innocent but it's too late now), and searching for "Devil's marks" (any mole, scar, or blemish could be proof of Satan's touch).

Hopkins and men like him created economies of persecution. Towns paid them to identify witches. They had every incentive to find as many as possible. They developed techniques that guaranteed confessions. And they wrapped their profitable murder in legal procedure and righteous language.

The Devil had created a system where killing women was a legitimate profession, where torture was standard legal procedure, where due process guaranteed conviction, and where the machinery of state power was deployed not to protect people but to exterminate them.

The Geography of Horror: Where the Devil's Work Flourished

The witch hunts weren't evenly distributed across Europe. Germany saw the highest number of executions—approximately 42% of all witch hunt deaths occurred there. Particular regions became killing fields: the Bamberg witch trials (1626-1631) resulted in over 600 executions. The Würzburg witch trials (1626-1631) killed approximately 900 people. In the city of Trier, witch trials between 1581 and 1593 resulted in 368 executions.

What made some regions particularly brutal? Often it was political fragmentation. In areas with strong centralized authority (like Spain with its Inquisition, ironically), there were checks on local persecution—central authorities could review cases, question procedures, limit torture. But in fragmented regions like Germany, with numerous small princedoms and jurisdictions, local authorities could persecute without oversight.

The Devil's strategy was clear: exploit political chaos, work through local authorities, prevent centralized review, allow persecution to flourish in pockets where no one would stop it.

And it worked. For centuries, it worked.

THE DEVIL thus fulfilled his role in the witch hunts by creating legal machinery that guaranteed conviction (torture, spectral evidence, anonymous accusation), professionalizing persecution (the witch-finders and their incentives), and exploiting political fragmentation (allowing local killing fields to operate without oversight).

• • •

Evidence for the Prosecution: MAN

If God provided justification and the Devil provided legal machinery, Man provided the violence. In every town, in every witch hunt, it was men who denounced, men who arrested, men who tortured, men who judged, men who executed. The witch hunts were male violence enacted on female bodies, backed by male authority in church and state.

Men as Accusers

While both men and women made witch-craft accusations, the system was designed and controlled by men. Male authorities decided which accusations to pursue, which accusations had merit, which women would be arrested and tried.

Men accused women for refusing sexual advances. Men accused wives they wanted to be rid of. Men accused widows whose property they coveted. Men accused women who had rejected them, embarrassed them, challenged them, or simply annoyed them. The witch hunts gave individual men the power to eliminate any woman they wanted gone.

Consider: a wealthy widow refuses to marry the man who wants her property. He accuses her of witchcraft. She's arrested. Under torture, she confesses. She's executed. He claims her property. Legal murder for personal profit, blessed by the Church and sanctioned by law.

Or: a woman rebuffs a man's sexual demands. He spreads rumors that she's a witch. Neighbors remember strange occurrences—someone's cow died last year, someone's child was sick last month—maybe it was her witchcraft? She's accused. She's arrested. Under torture, she confesses. She burns. The message is clear: submit sexually or risk burning.

The witch hunts were terrorism. They created an environment where any woman, anywhere, for any reason, could be accused, convicted, and killed. Every woman knew this. Every woman lived with this terror. And that terror served its purpose: women stayed quiet, stayed submissive, stayed inside male control.

Men as Torturers and Executioners

The torture was detailed, systematic, and brutal. Methods included:

The strappado: hang the accused by her wrists tied behind her back, dislocating shoulders. Add weights to increase the agony.

The rack: stretch the body until joints dislocate and ligaments tear.

Thumbscrews: crush fingers and thumbs in metal vises.

The boots: crush legs in metal boots that could be tightened until bones shattered.

Sleep deprivation: keep the accused awake for days until she was delirious.

The swimming test: bind and throw into water to see if she floats (guilty) or drowns (innocent but dead).

Searching for Devil's marks: strip the woman naked, shave all her body hair, examine every inch of her body for moles or marks, prick suspected marks with needles to see if they bleed (if they do, innocent; if they don't, guilty).

These procedures were carried out by men on women's bodies. Men stripped women naked. Men examined their bodies. Men inflicted the pain. Men controlled when it stopped—and it stopped only when the woman confessed or died.

The sexual violence inherent in these procedures is obvious. Strip a woman, examine her naked body in detail, penetrate her with instruments (the needles searching for Devil's marks), cause her agony while she's helpless—this was sexual torture disguised as legal procedure.

And then the executions: burning alive (the most common method), hanging, beheading, drowning. Men built the pyres. Men lit the fires. Men watched women burn, listened to them scream, saw them die in agony. And they called this holy work.

Men as Beneficiaries

Men profited from the witch hunts in every possible way:

Materially: Accused witches' property was confiscated. Widows with land, women with businesses, any woman with assets—once accused and convicted, her property went to the state, to the Church, or to her male relatives. The witch hunts were profitable.

Professionally: Witch-finders, judges, torturers, executioners all earned money. The trials required lawyers, clerks, guards. An entire economy of persecution developed, all staffed by men, all profiting from women's deaths.

Socially: Eliminating "difficult" women, independent women, women who challenged male authority served every man who wanted women properly submissive. The terror kept women in line.

Sexually: The witch hunts gave men power over women's bodies. The torture included forced nudity, bodily examination, penetration with instruments. The trials featured detailed interrogation about women's sexual behavior. The entire process was saturated with male sexual violence against women.

Psychologically: Men got to be heroes. Saving their communities from Satan's agents. Doing God's work. Protecting Christian civilization. The witch hunts allowed men to enact brutal violence against women while feeling righteous about it.

MAN thus fulfilled his role in the witch hunts by making accusations (targeting women who refused submission or whom he wanted eliminated), inflicting torture (stripping, examining, and torturing women's bodies), carrying out executions (burning women alive), and profiting from persecution (materially, professionally, socially, sexually, and psychologically).

• • •

The Numbers Are Not Abstract

Let us be clear about what we're discussing. Conservative estimates suggest 40,000-60,000 executions over 300 years. Some scholars estimate as many as 100,000. Roughly 75-85% were women.

This means somewhere between 30,000 and 85,000 women were executed for witchcraft in Europe between 1450 and 1750.

But these numbers are just executions—just the women who were actually killed. For every woman executed, many more were accused, arrested, imprisoned, tortured, and released (if they survived). The psychological terror affected every woman. The message was universal: you could be next.

In some regions, the killing was concentrated and brutal. In the Würzburg witch trials, entire families were executed—children as young as seven were burned as witches. In some German towns, the adult female population was significantly depleted by witch hunts. Women simply disappeared, burned to death because someone accused them of causing a storm or making someone sick or having sex with demons.

These weren't statistics. They were human beings. Women who had names, lives, families, knowledge, skills, dreams. Midwives who had safely delivered hundreds of babies. Herbalists who had healed countless sick people. Widows living quietly on their small plots of land. Young women who said no to the wrong man. Old women who were too sharp-tongued. Mothers, daughters, sisters, friends.

Stripped naked. Tortured until they confessed to impossible crimes. Burned alive while crowds watched.

This was the Masculine Triad's answer to women's resistance: mass murder, legally sanctioned, religiously blessed, and enacted by individual men across Europe for three centuries.

• • •

Why the Witch Hunts Ended

The witch hunts didn't end because men suddenly became enlightened about women's humanity. They didn't end because the Church realized that burning women was wrong. They didn't end because women successfully resisted.

They ended because the Enlightenment brought new forms of supposed rationality that made witch hunting seem superstitious and backward. The same intellectual movement that would declare all men equal (while keeping women subordinate) decided that belief in witches was beneath the dignity of rational men. Not that women didn't deserve persecution—just that witchcraft was an insufficiently scientific justification for it.

The persecution didn't stop. It merely changed form. As we shall see in subsequent chapters, the Masculine Triad would find new ways to subordinate women, new justifications for controlling them, new methods of maintaining power. The methods would become more subtle, more "rational," more disguised. But the purpose would remain the same.

The witch hunts stand as proof of what the Masculine Triad is capable of when women threaten male control. When legal erasure, economic dependence, and domestic violence prove insufficient, when women still claim independence and knowledge and power despite everything the system does to break them—the Triad will kill them.

Tens of thousands of women burned. Their crime? Existing outside male control. Their punishment? Death by fire, blessed by God, sanctioned by law, enacted by men.

Remember this when anyone tells you that historical oppression wasn't "that bad." Remember this when anyone suggests that women have always been protected and cherished by men. Remember this when anyone claims that women's subordination was natural or inevitable or benign.

The pyres tell a different story. The ashes bear witness. The Masculine Triad, when threatened, will burn.

CHAPTER SEVEN

Joan of Arc and the Dangerous Woman

On May 30, 1431, in the marketplace of Rouen, a nineteen-year-old peasant girl was burned alive. Joan of Arc—who had led French armies to victory, who had crowned a king, who had claimed to hear the voices of saints directing her actions—was tied to a stake and set on fire. She screamed the name of Jesus as the flames consumed her. The executioner later testified that he had never felt such remorse for any execution he had carried out.

Joan's crime, officially, was relapsing into heresy. The specific heresy? Wearing men's clothing.

Let that sink in. A woman who had led armies, who had changed the course of a war, who had exercised military and political authority reserved exclusively for men, who had claimed direct communication with God bypassing the male Church hierarchy entirely—this woman was burned alive for wearing pants.

The absurdity is the point. The Masculine Triad needed a legal justification to kill her, and they seized on the one charge they could make stick: cross-dressing, prohibited in Deuteronomy. But the real crime wasn't what she wore. The real crime was what she *was*: a woman claiming authority independent of male control.

Joan of Arc represents the most dangerous thing a woman could be in the medieval world—a woman who bypassed the entire system of male domination. She didn't ask permission. She didn't submit to fathers, husbands, priests, or kings. She claimed authority directly from God and wielded it in the most masculine sphere imaginable: warfare. And for this, she had to die.

Her trial and execution reveal the Masculine Triad's playbook when faced with a woman who cannot be controlled through normal means. When a woman steps so far outside the boundaries, when she claims power so completely, the Triad's only response is elimination.

• • •

The Impossible Woman

To understand why Joan was so threatening, we must understand what she represented. She was an illiterate peasant girl from a tiny village in northeastern France. She had no education, no noble blood, no family connections, no wealth, no status. By every metric the medieval world used to measure power, she had none.

Yet in 1429, at age seventeen, she presented herself at the court of the Dauphin Charles and convinced him—against all advice from his counselors—to give her soldiers and allow her to lead them to lift the siege of Orléans. She did. The English, who had been winning the Hundred Years' War decisively, suffered a devastating defeat. Joan then led the French army through a series of victories culminating in Charles's coronation at Reims.

A teenage peasant girl with no military training had done what experienced commanders could not do. She had turned the tide of a war that had been going badly for France for generations. She had made a king.

How? She claimed she heard voices—specifically, the voices of Saint Michael, Saint Catherine, and Saint Margaret. These voices, she testified, told her that God had chosen her to save France. She was to dress in men's clothing, lead armies, drive out the English, and crown Charles as the rightful king of France.

And she did it. Not metaphorically. Not symbolically. Actually, tangibly, militarily did it.

This was intolerable. A woman—uneducated, poor, young— claiming direct divine authority and exercising military and political power? Every element of this threatened the Masculine Triad's fundamental organizing principles.

Bypassing Male Religious Authority

Joan claimed she received her instructions directly from God via the saints. She did not need priests to interpret Scripture for her. She did not need the Church to mediate between her and the divine. She did not need any male authority to validate her divine mission. God spoke to her —a woman—directly.

This was heresy in the most threatening sense. The entire structure of the medieval Church rested on the premise that the clergy— exclusively male—were the necessary intermediaries between God and humanity. Priests heard confessions, administered sacraments, interpreted Scripture, and conveyed God's will to the faithful. The Church's power depended on maintaining this monopoly on divine communication.

Joan shattered this monopoly. If God could speak directly to an illiterate peasant girl, what was the Church for? If a woman could hear divine voices and act on them without clerical approval, what happened to male spiritual authority? If Joan's mission was genuinely from God—and her military success suggested it might be—then the Church's claim that women were spiritually inferior and unsuited for divine communication was exposed as a lie.

This was why the trial focused so intensely on her voices. The prosecutors needed to prove that her voices were demonic, not divine. If they were divine, then everything the Church taught about women's spiritual incapacity was wrong. If they were demonic, then Joan could be condemned as a witch or heretic and burned.

Exercising Male Political and Military Authority

Joan led armies. She wore armor. She carried a banner into battle. She made military decisions. She commanded soldiers—men—who obeyed her. She exercised authority in the most quintessentially masculine domain: warfare.

This was not a woman advising from the sidelines or influencing events through manipulation of male relatives. This was a woman in armor, on horseback, at the head of an army, making tactical decisions and leading charges. She fought. She bled. She commanded.

The medieval social order could not accommodate this. Women were excluded from military service, from bearing arms, from commanding men, from exercising political authority. These were male spheres, defined as male precisely because they required the strength, courage, rationality, and divine favor that women allegedly lacked.

Joan proved this was nonsense. A teenage girl with no training could lead armies successfully. A woman could exercise military authority and men would follow her. A female could possess the courage, tactical insight, and leadership that supposedly belonged only to males.

Her very existence invalidated the justifications for male monopoly on political and military power. If Joan could do it, what was the argument for excluding all other women? If God chose a woman for this mission, what did that say about claims that God intended men to rule?

Refusing Subordination to Any Man

Joan was unmarried. She had left her family home without her parents' permission. She lived among soldiers. She refused to submit to the Bishop's authority during her trial. She insisted that she would obey God alone, not the Church.

She existed entirely outside the structures of male control. She had no husband governing her. She had disobeyed her father. She rejected Church authority. She commanded men rather than being commanded by them. She was, in every possible way, an ungoverned woman.

The medieval system could not tolerate ungoverned women. Every woman was supposed to be under the authority of some man—father, husband, brother, priest. A woman outside male control was dangerous, potentially chaotic, certainly unnatural.

Joan was not merely outside male control—she inverted it. Men followed her orders. Kings sought her counsel. Bishops interrogated her, and she refused to submit to their authority, insisting that God's authority superseded theirs.

This was revolutionary. This was terrifying. This had to be stopped.

• • •

Evidence for the Prosecution: GOD

The Church orchestrated Joan's trial and execution. This was not a secular affair—it was an ecclesiastical court, trying her for religious crimes, under Church law. Priests interrogated her. Theologians judged her. The Church condemned her. The Church's role in her destruction was central and damning.

The Theological Impossibility of Female Divine Authority

The Church had taught for centuries that women were spiritually inferior. Aquinas had declared them defective and misbegotten. Paul had commanded them to be silent in churches. The entire theological edifice of Christianity rested on female subordination to male spiritual authority.

Joan's claim that God spoke to her directly threatened this edifice. If God could speak to a woman, if God could choose a woman for a divine mission, if God could grant a woman authority over men—then every theological argument for female subordination was wrong.

The Church could not allow this. They could not admit that Joan's voices were genuine divine communication because that admission would destroy the theological justification for male spiritual monopoly. So they had to prove her voices were demonic.

The trial interrogators pressed her repeatedly about her voices. How did she know they were from God? How did they appear to her? What did they say? Why would God choose her, a mere woman, for such a mission?

Joan's answers were brilliant and frustrating to her interrogators. When asked if she was in God's grace, she replied: "If I am not, may God put me there; and if I am, may God so keep me." This was a perfect answer—if she claimed to be in grace, she was presumptuous; if she claimed not to be, she was admitting sin. Her response avoided the trap entirely.

When pressed on why God would choose a woman, she simply stated that it pleased God to do so. She claimed no special worthiness, only that God had chosen her and she had obeyed. This was theologically unassailable—God's will was God's will, and humans had no standing to question it.

But the Church would not accept this. They insisted she submit her visions to the Church's judgment. Let the clergy determine if her voices were divine or demonic. Let male theological authority pronounce on the validity of her divine communication.

Joan refused. She stated that she would be judged by God alone. The voices told her what to do, and she had obeyed. She would not submit to the Church's judgment on what God had told her directly.

This refusal was her death warrant. The Church could not tolerate a woman claiming authority independent of clerical mediation. If they allowed Joan to maintain that her divine mission superseded Church authority, they opened the door for any woman to claim divine inspiration and reject male spiritual control.

The Cross-Dressing Charge: When Theology Becomes Absurd

Joan faced seventy charges initially. These were whittled down to twelve, which included claims that her visions were demonic, that she prophesied future events, that she refused to submit to Church authority, and that she wore men's clothing.

The clothing charge seems almost comically trivial compared to the others. Leading armies against God's anointed English? Fine, apparently. Claiming divine visions? Concerning but not conclusive. Refusing Church authority? Troubling but hard to prove definitively.

But wearing pants? That they could prove. That violated a clear biblical prohibition in Deuteronomy. That was visible, undeniable, persistent. And critically, that was something they could use to execute her legally.

The logic was tortured: Joan agreed under threat of immediate burning to sign an abjuration renouncing her visions and promising not to wear men's clothing anymore. She signed—possibly without fully understanding what she was signing, given she was illiterate. She was given women's clothing and her death sentence was commuted to life in prison.

Four days later, she was found wearing men's clothing again. She explained that her guards had taken her women's clothing and given her only men's clothing—some witnesses later testified that guards had stolen her dress while she slept, forcing her to wear male clothes to use the latrine. She also testified that guards had attempted to rape her, and she wore men's clothing tied tightly for protection.

None of this mattered. She had "relapsed" into wearing men's clothing. Under Inquisition rules, someone who relapsed into condemned behavior after abjuring it could be executed as an unrepentant heretic. The Church had her.

On May 30, 1431, Joan was burned alive for wearing pants.

The absurdity reveals the truth: the Church didn't care about her clothing. They cared about eliminating a woman who had claimed authority independent of male control. The clothing charge was simply the legal mechanism they used to kill her.

God's Vengeance: Posthumous Exoneration

Twenty-five years after Joan's execution, the Church retried her posthumously and declared the original verdict null and void. They proclaimed her innocent of all charges. In 1920, the Church canonized her as a saint.

This reversal is telling. If Joan was a heretic and witch deserving of burning in 1431, how did she become a saint in 1920? The facts didn't change. What changed was who controlled the narrative and which outcome served Church interests.

In 1431, the English-allied Church faction needed her dead to discredit Charles VII. In 1456, Charles had won the war and needed Joan's mission validated to legitimize his rule. In 1920, the Church needed national heroes and patriotic symbols.

Joan's sanctity was always political. Her condemnation was political. Her execution was political. The Church used God's name to burn her when that served their purposes, and used God's name to sanctify her when that served their purposes.

The Church thus fulfilled GOD's role in Joan's destruction by denying the possibility of female divine authority (insisting her voices be submitted to male judgment), using religious law to execute her (the cross-dressing charge and relapse doctrine), and later sanctifying her when politically convenient (demonstrating the political nature of the entire proceeding).

• • •

Evidence for the Prosecution: THE DEVIL

The trial itself was the Devil's work—not the trial as religious proceeding, but the trial as legal machinery designed to guarantee conviction and provide a veneer of legitimacy to political murder.

The Corrupt Proceedings

Joan's trial was a mockery of justice. Bishop Pierre Cauchon, who orchestrated it, had personal and political reasons to want her dead. Joan had captured the Beauvais province during her military campaigns—Cauchon was the Bishop of Beauvais. She had championed Charles VII—Cauchon supported the English and Burgundian cause. He was not an impartial judge; he was a prosecutor, judge, and executioner rolled into one.

The trial violated numerous procedural norms. Joan was held in a secular English prison rather than an ecclesiastical one, despite being tried by a Church court. She was guarded by English soldiers who harassed her and attempted to rape her. She was denied access to counsel. She was interrogated for hours by teams of trained theologians while exhausted, isolated, and threatened with torture and execution.

The proceedings were designed to produce a guilty verdict. When Joan gave answers that were theologically sound or avoided traps, the interrogators simply kept pressing until they found something they could use. When she successfully defended her divine mission, they pivoted to her clothing. When that seemed insufficient, they threatened her with torture.

The trial record itself was manipulated. Guillaume Manchon, the chief notary, later testified that Cauchon had altered the transcript to make Joan appear more guilty. Statements she made in her defense were omitted or changed. The record was a lie from the start.

The Trap of the Abjuration

The abjuration Joan signed was legal entrapment. On May 24, she was taken to a public scaffold and told she would be burned immediately unless she renounced her visions and signed a document promising to obey the Church and stop wearing men's clothing. Faced with immediate execution by fire, she signed—a document she likely couldn't read.

The purpose of the abjuration was not to save Joan's soul. It was to create the legal mechanism for her execution. If she kept the promises in the abjuration, she would rot in prison for life. If she broke them—and they would ensure she broke them—they could execute her as a relapsed heretic.

And they did ensure she broke them. Joan's guards took her women's clothing and gave her only men's clothing. When she needed to leave her cell to use the latrine, she had to wear the male clothes. When she complained, the guards refused to return her dress. Some witnesses testified that she was given literally no choice—it was wear the male clothes or remain naked.

Four days after her abjuration, Cauchon was notified that Joan was wearing men's clothes again. He came immediately to her cell with other clerics. Joan explained that guards had taken her female clothing and she had no choice. She also said that her voices had told her she had done wrong to abjure out of fear of the fire, and that she would not deny them again.

This was enough. She had "relapsed." She could now be legally executed.

The entire sequence was a setup. Force her to abjure under threat of immediate death. Take away her ability to comply with the abjuration. Declare her a relapsed heretic when she inevitably wore the male clothes. Burn her.

Legal murder, dressed up as justice.

The Political Motivation

Joan's trial was never about heresy. It was about discrediting Charles VII. If Joan was a heretic and witch, then her mission to crown Charles was demonic. If she was working for Satan, then Charles's coronation—which she had orchestrated—was illegitimate. If Charles's coronation was illegitimate, then he was not the rightful king of France, and the English claim to the throne stood.

This is why the English paid for the trial. This is why they insisted she be tried rather than treated as a prisoner of war. This is why Cauchon—a French bishop loyal to the English cause—was chosen to lead the proceedings. This is why the University of Paris, which supported English claims to France, provided the theological backing.

Joan had to be condemned for heresy to invalidate Charles's kingship. Her execution was a political necessity disguised as religious judgment. The Devil's specialty: making murder look like law, making political assassination look like justice.

THE DEVIL thus fulfilled his role in Joan's destruction by creating corrupt legal proceedings (biased judge, manipulated transcript, denied counsel), setting legal traps (the abjuration and relapse mechanism), and serving political purposes (discrediting Charles VII by condemning Joan as a heretic).

• • •

Evidence for the Prosecution: MAN

Individual men—with names, faces, choices—condemned and killed Joan of Arc. They were not abstractions. They were human beings who chose to participate in her destruction, and they did so to preserve male power.

The Men Who Interrogated Her

Pierre Cauchon, Bishop of Beauvais, orchestrated the trial. He selected the assessors who would judge her. He controlled the proceedings. He manipulated the transcript. When the trial seemed in danger of not producing a guilty verdict, he threatened and cajoled. He was not seeking truth or justice—he was seeking Joan's death.

Jean d'Estivet, the promoter (prosecutor) of the trial, interrogated Joan with particular viciousness. He called her a whore, a blasphemer, and worse. He pressed her on sexual matters, asking if she was a virgin, if she had consorted with men, if her voices had appeared to her naked. The sexual harassment was relentless.

Dozens of theologians from the University of Paris participated as assessors, asking questions designed to trap her. They were learned men, educated in theology and law, interrogating an illiterate teenager. The power imbalance was stark, and they exploited it ruthlessly.

Not all participants were equally culpable—some later expressed regret, some testified at the rehabilitation trial about the trial's corruption. But many were willing collaborators in a legal murder, and they did it to preserve male ecclesiastical and political authority.

The Men Who Imprisoned Her

Joan was held in an English military prison, guarded by English soldiers. These guards subjected her to constant harassment. She testified that guards had attempted to rape her—she wore the male clothing tied tightly even while sleeping for protection against sexual assault.

Multiple witnesses at the rehabilitation trial testified that an English nobleman attempted to rape Joan in her cell. She fought him off. The guards did nothing to protect her—they were part of the threat.

After Joan signed the abjuration promising not to wear men's clothing, the guards took her women's clothing and gave her only male clothes. When she asked for her dress back, they refused. They created the situation that led to her "relapse."

These men had her in their power—young, alone, chained in a cell. They could have treated her as a prisoner of war with some measure of respect. Instead, they harassed her, threatened her sexually, and set her up for execution. And they did this because she was a woman who had dared to command them and their compatriots in battle.

The Men Who Executed Her

On May 30, 1431, in the marketplace of Rouen, men tied Joan to a stake. Men piled wood around her. Men lit the fire. Men watched as a nineteen-year-old woman screamed in agony as the flames consumed her.

The executioner later testified that he felt extraordinary remorse—but he did it anyway. He could have refused. He could have bungled the execution. He could have shown mercy by strangling her before the fire reached her (a common mercy for condemned prisoners). He did none of these things.

English soldiers gathered to watch. They had orders to prevent anyone from retrieving her body—her ashes were to be thrown in the Seine to prevent her becoming a martyr with relics. Men ensured that even in death, Joan would be erased.

The executioner reportedly said he had never felt such remorse for an execution. But men did it anyway. Because preserving male authority—the authority of the Church, the crown, the military, the social order—was more important than the life of one extraordinary woman.

Why Joan Had to Die

Joan had to die because she proved that women could do everything men claimed only men could do. She could receive divine revelation without male intermediaries. She could lead armies. She could exercise political authority. She could command men. She could be courageous, strategic, charismatic, and effective.

If Joan could do all this, then the entire justification for male monopoly on power collapsed. If a teenage peasant girl with no education or training could lead armies to victory, what was the argument for excluding all women from military and political authority? If God spoke directly to a woman, why did women need male priests to mediate between them and the divine?

Joan was a living refutation of everything the Masculine Triad taught about female incapacity. And the Triad's response was to kill her and call it justice.

MAN thus fulfilled his role in Joan's destruction by personally interrogating and condemning her (Cauchon and the assessors), sexually threatening and setting her up for relapse (the guards), and carrying out her execution (the executioner and soldiers).

• • •

The Pattern of Destruction

Joan's trial and execution were not unique—they were exemplary. They demonstrate the Masculine Triad's standard response to women who claim authority independent of male control:

First, deny the possibility. Women cannot receive divine revelation, cannot lead armies, cannot exercise authority. If a woman claims to do these things, she must be lying, delusional, or demonic.

Second, if denial fails because the woman's success is undeniable, attack her femininity. She must not be a real woman—she dresses like a man, lives like a man, behaves like a man. Real women are submissive, domestic, silent. This woman is unnatural, monstrous.

Third, if attacks on her femininity fail to discredit her, use law to destroy her. Find some technical violation—in Joan's case, cross-dressing. Build a legal case around it. Create traps that guarantee conviction. Make murder look like justice.

Fourth, execute her. Eliminate the threat. And do it publicly, brutally, in a way that terrorizes other women who might dare to follow her example.

This pattern appears again and again throughout history when women claim power. The details change—sometimes the charge is witchcraft, sometimes heresy, sometimes sexual immorality, sometimes "unnatural" behavior. But the pattern is constant: deny, defeminize, delegitimize, destroy.

The Message to All Women

Joan's execution was meant to send a message. Women who step outside their ordained roles will be destroyed. Women who claim authority independent of male control will be eliminated. Women who bypass the male hierarchy—religious, political, or social—will burn.

The message was clear: stay in your place. Submit to fathers, husbands, priests, kings. Do not claim divine authority. Do not exercise political or military power. Do not command men. Do not dress as you please. Do not exist outside male control.

Or burn.

And the message worked. For centuries after Joan's death, she was remembered not as a hero but as a cautionary tale. A woman who stepped out of line and suffered the consequences. It would be nearly five hundred years before she would be rehabilitated, sanctified, and claimed as a national hero.

But even her eventual sanctification cannot erase what was done to her. A nineteen-year-old woman who had saved her country was tied to a stake and burned alive by the combined forces of Church and state because she had dared to claim authority that belonged, supposedly, only to men.

• • •

The Unlearned Lesson

We like to tell Joan's story as a tragedy with a happy ending. She was wrongly condemned but eventually vindicated. She was killed as a heretic but proclaimed a saint. Justice, delayed, was done.

But this narrative obscures the truth. Joan died screaming in flames. Her vindication came twenty-five years too late to save her. Her sanctification came five centuries too late to matter to her. The men who killed her suffered no consequences. Cauchon died of natural causes, still a bishop. The guards who harassed her went unpunished. The executioner expressed remorse but collected his fee.

And the system that killed her continued unchanged. The Church continued to exclude women from authority. States continued to deny women political power. The Masculine Triad continued to subordinate women through law, religion, and violence.

Joan's story teaches us that the Masculine Triad will kill to preserve its power. When a woman becomes too dangerous—when she claims too much authority, demonstrates too much competence, threatens too directly the narrative of male superiority—the Triad will eliminate her.

They will use whatever tools are available: religious law, secular law, accusations of heresy, charges of witchcraft, claims of unnatural behavior. They will manipulate legal proceedings, coerce confessions, manufacture evidence. They will do whatever it takes to destroy the woman who dares to challenge male supremacy.

And they will call it justice.

Joan of Arc was murdered by the Masculine Triad because she proved that everything the Triad taught about women was a lie. She proved women could receive divine revelation, lead armies, exercise authority, and command men. She proved it so conclusively that the only response was to kill her.

Her ashes were thrown in the Seine. But her example lived on—a testament to what women could do, and a warning about what men would do to stop them.

The Masculine Triad had burned her body. But they could not burn the truth she embodied: women were capable of everything men claimed only they could do. And men would kill to keep that truth from spreading.

PART III: THE MODERN TRIAD

CHAPTER EIGHT

The Enlightenment's Exclusion

The Enlightenment promised to liberate humanity from the chains of superstition, tradition, and arbitrary authority. Beginning in the late seventeenth century and reaching its peak in the eighteenth, this intellectual revolution proclaimed that reason—not faith, not tradition, not the accident of birth—should govern human affairs. All men were created equal. All men possessed natural rights. All men could use their rational faculties to understand the world and improve their condition.

All *men*.

The Enlightenment was perhaps the most consequential intellectual movement in Western history. It produced the American and French Revolutions. It laid the philosophical foundation for modern democracy, human rights, and constitutional government. It challenged the divine right of kings, the authority of the Church, and the rigid class structures of the old regime. It proclaimed that human beings were born free and equal, endowed with inalienable rights.

And it explicitly, deliberately, systematically excluded women.

This was not oversight. This was not incomplete application of universal principles that later thinkers would extend to women. This was the deliberate exclusion of half of humanity from the category of rational beings deserving of rights and freedom. The greatest minds of the Enlightenment—Locke, Rousseau, Kant, Voltaire, Montesquieu—expended considerable intellectual energy explaining why their magnificent theories of human liberty did not apply to women.

The Enlightenment replaced the divine authority of God and Church with the secular authority of Reason. But Reason, as defined by Enlightenment philosophers, was male. Women, by nature, lacked the capacity for rational thought that entitled human beings to liberty and equality. They were creatures of emotion, sensation, and appetite—incapable of the reasoned deliberation that citizenship and autonomy required.

The Masculine Triad adapted. If the medieval system subordinated women through religious authority, legal erasure, and household control, the Enlightenment system would subordinate them through a new ideology: the scientific, rational, philosophically grounded claim that women were naturally inferior to men. The chains would look different—more civilized, more rational, more based on "nature" rather than divine command. But they would still be chains.

• • •

The Promise and the Betrayal

To understand the magnitude of the Enlightenment's betrayal, we must first understand what it promised. Enlightenment thinkers proclaimed principles so radical, so revolutionary, that they overturned millennia of political and social organization:

All human beings are born equal. There is no natural hierarchy that places some people above others by accident of birth. Kings are not inherently superior to commoners. Nobles are not inherently superior to peasants. One person's humanity is worth exactly as much as another's.

Human beings possess natural rights. Before any government, before any law, before any social contract, human beings have rights that no authority can legitimately violate. Life, liberty, property, the pursuit of happiness—these belong to human beings simply because they are human.

Reason is the supreme authority. Not the Church. Not tradition. Not the King. Human reason can discern truth, discover natural laws, and organize society on rational principles. Authority is legitimate only when it can be justified by reason.

Self-governance is the right of rational beings. Since reason is universal and no human being is naturally subordinate to another, people have the right to govern themselves. Democracy, republicanism, constitutional government—these follow logically from the premise that rational beings should not be subject to arbitrary rule.

These principles were revolutionary. They undermined the entire structure of European society—the divine right of kings, the hereditary privileges of the aristocracy, the authority of the Church over political and intellectual life. Enlightenment ideas would inspire revolutions on two continents and establish the philosophical foundation for modern liberal democracy.

But when it came to women, these principles suddenly stopped applying.

All human beings are born equal—except women, who are born subordinate to men by nature.

Human beings possess natural rights—except women, whose rights are subsumed into their fathers' or husbands'.

Reason is the supreme authority—but women lack the capacity for reason that would make them authorities over anything, including their own lives.

Self-governance is the right of rational beings—but women are not fully rational, so they require male governance.

The Enlightenment didn't ignore women. It actively theorized their exclusion. The great philosophers devoted considerable attention to explaining why the universal principles they championed were not, in fact, universal.

• • •

Evidence for the Prosecution: GOD

The Enlightenment partially displaced traditional religious authority—but only partially. And where religious teachings about women could be reframed as "natural" observations, they retained their power. The Enlightenment's new "God" was Nature, and Nature, as interpreted by male philosophers, had ordained female subordination just as surely as the old God had.

From Divine Command to Natural Order

Medieval theology had justified female subordination through Scripture and divine command. God created Eve from Adam's rib. God punished Eve for the Fall by placing her under Adam's authority.

God spoke through Paul to command women's silence and submission. These were not arguments to be debated but divine orders to be obeyed.

The Enlightenment rejected this approach—in theory. Rational inquiry, not scriptural authority, should determine truth. Human nature, observable through reason and experience, should guide social organization.

But the conclusions remained remarkably similar. Where the Church had said "God commands women to submit," Enlightenment philosophers said "Nature designs women for submission." Where theology had declared women's intellectual inferiority as divine punishment for Eve's sin, philosophy declared it as natural fact, observable through scientific reason.

The theological claims hadn't been disproven. They had been translated. Female subordination was no longer God's will; it was Nature's design. And Nature, conveniently, wanted exactly what male theologians had always said God wanted: women silent, submissive, domestic, and under male authority.

The Secular Theology of Separate Spheres

Enlightenment philosophy developed what would become the "doctrine of separate spheres"—the idea that men and women were naturally suited for different domains. Men belonged in the public sphere: politics, commerce, intellectual life, civic engagement. Women belonged in the private sphere: home, family, domestic duties, child-rearing.

This wasn't presented as oppression. It was presented as natural complementarity. Men and women were different but equal—each had their proper sphere, each was suited to their domain, each fulfilled their nature in their designated role. The man who ruled in public and the woman who ruled in the home were supposedly equal partners.

But of course they weren't equal. The public sphere had power, influence, resources, and recognition. The private sphere had none of these. Men made laws that governed women. Women had no voice in making laws that governed men. Men controlled property, commerce, education, and politics. Women controlled nothing—their labor, their bodies, their children all belonged legally to their husbands.

The "separate spheres" ideology was medieval coverture dressed in Enlightenment clothes. It still erased women from public life. It still subordinated women to male authority. It simply offered a new justification: not "God commands it" but "Nature designed it."

The Enlightenment's religious innovation was not to reject the theological framework for female subordination but to secularize it. The new god—Nature—spoke through philosophers instead of priests, and the new scripture—scientific observation—was interpreted by men who, remarkably, kept finding exactly what the old scripture had said: women were meant to submit.

• • •

Evidence for the Prosecution: THE DEVIL

The Devil's work in the Enlightenment was to build the intellectual and legal structures that would exclude women from the new freedoms being won. As democracies replaced monarchies, as written constitutions replaced arbitrary royal authority, as "the rights of man" became the organizing principle of political life—women were systematically excluded from all of it.

The Philosophers Who Theorized Exclusion

Jean-Jacques Rousseau (1712-1778), perhaps the most influential Enlightenment philosopher on questions of education and human development, devoted considerable attention to explaining why women should be educated for subordination. His treatise *Emile* (1762) described the ideal education for a boy—free, natural, developing his rational faculties—and then, in Book V, described the ideal education for Sophie, Emile's future wife.

Sophie's education was entirely different. Where Emile learned to think independently, Sophie learned to please. Where Emile developed his reason, Sophie developed her charm. Where Emile was trained for autonomy, Sophie was trained for obedience.

Rousseau was explicit about why:

> *"The whole education of women ought to be relative to men. To please them, to be useful to them, to make themselves loved and honored by them, to educate them when young, to care for them when grown, to counsel them, to console them, and to make life agreeable and sweet to them—these are the duties of women at all times, and should be taught them from their infancy."*

Women existed, in Rousseau's view, to serve men. Their education should prepare them for this service, not for independent thought or action. A woman who developed her reason would be unwomanly, unnatural, unfit for her proper role.

Rousseau went further. He argued that women should care primarily about reputation—about what others thought of them—

while men should care about virtue itself. For men, "opinion is the grave of virtue." For women, opinion "is its throne." A woman's worth depended entirely on others' perceptions; she had no independent moral standing.

This was the philosopher who wrote *The Social Contract*, arguing that legitimate government requires the consent of the governed. But women were not part of "the governed" in any meaningful sense—they were governed by men, through men, for men's benefit. The social contract was a contract among men about how to govern women.

Kant's Incomplete Enlightenment

Immanuel Kant (1724-1804) famously defined Enlightenment as "man's emergence from his self-imposed immaturity." He urged humanity to "dare to know," to think for themselves, to reject dependence on external authorities. His moral philosophy proclaimed the dignity of every rational being and the categorical imperative to treat humanity never merely as a means but always as an end.

But Kant explicitly excluded women from this project of enlightenment. In his *Observations on the Feeling of the Beautiful and Sublime* (1764), he wrote:

> *"Laborious learning or painful pondering, even if a woman should greatly succeed in it, destroy the merits that are proper to her sex, and because of their rarity they can make of her an object of cold admiration; but at the same time they will weaken the charms with which she exercises her great power over the other sex."*

A woman who developed her intellect destroyed what made her a woman. Her "charms"—her attractiveness to men—were incompatible with learning and thought. A woman might as well grow a beard, Kant suggested, as become a serious scholar.

In his essay "What is Enlightenment?" (1784), Kant proclaimed that no one currently achieved enlightenment—but he specifically noted that no *women* were enlightened. Scholars have debated whether this was descriptive (women happen not to be enlightened) or prescriptive (women cannot be enlightened by nature). But the practical effect was the same: the great project of human liberation through reason excluded half of humanity.

Kant's moral philosophy, with its universal categorical imperative applying to all rational beings, should have implied women's equality. If the moral law applies to all rational beings, and if women are rational beings, then women are moral equals deserving of respect and autonomy. But Kant seemed to doubt whether women were fully rational in the relevant sense. Their virtue was "beautiful" rather than "noble." They avoided evil because it was ugly, not because it was wrong. They were governed by feeling rather than reason.

This was the philosopher who proclaimed human dignity inviolable, who argued that rational beings must never be treated merely as means, who grounded morality in the autonomy of the will.

And yet he could not extend these magnificent principles to women.

Locke's Contradictions

John Locke (1632-1704) is often credited with laying the philosophical foundations for liberal democracy. His *Two Treatises of Government* (1689) argued against the divine right of kings and for government by consent. His theory of the mind as a "blank slate" (*tabula rasa*) suggested that differences between people resulted from experience and education, not innate nature.

This should have led to advocacy for women's equality. If the mind is a blank slate, if differences result from education, then women's apparent intellectual inferiority is the product of their inferior education, not their inferior nature. Give women equal education and they will be equal.

Locke seemed to recognize this. He wrote that the notion of male superiority was "invented by men" and could theoretically be reversed. He thought women should be on "equal footing with men within a marriage." His blank slate theory was explicitly egalitarian about innate capacity.

Yet Locke also accepted that subordination was "apparently a woman's lot." He didn't challenge coverture, didn't advocate for women's political rights, didn't push for equal education. The revolutionary implications of his own theory stopped at the threshold of gender.

The Devil's philosophers created elaborate theoretical frameworks for human liberty—and equally elaborate explanations for why those frameworks excluded women. They argued for natural rights that women didn't possess, for rational autonomy that women couldn't achieve, for self-governance that women weren't capable of.

The Legal Exclusions

The new constitutions and legal codes that emerged from Enlightenment thought systematically excluded women. When the French National Assembly issued the Declaration of the Rights of Man and of the Citizen in 1789, the "man" was not a generic term for humanity. It meant men specifically. Women were not citizens. They had no political rights.

When Napoleon codified French law in 1804, the resulting Napoleonic Code became a model for legal systems across Europe and its colonies. It explicitly subordinated women to their husbands. Article 213 stated: "The husband owes protection to his wife; the wife owes obedience to her husband." Married women could not work without their husband's permission, could not control their own property, could not enter contracts, could not have custody of their children in divorce.

This was not medieval law surviving into the modern era. This was brand new law, drafted by Enlightenment-influenced legislators, explicitly designed to codify female subordination. The Napoleonic Code spread across Europe—to Italy, the Netherlands, Belgium, Spain, Portugal, and beyond—and to the European colonies around the world. It remained influential into the twentieth century.

The American Constitution, product of Enlightenment thought, did not grant women the right to vote. Women were not mentioned at all except in the provision that representatives would be apportioned based on "the whole Number of free Persons" (which included women for counting purposes but not for voting purposes). The Declaration of Independence proclaimed that "all men are created equal"—and meant men.

Coverture continued in English and American law. Married women remained legal non-entities, their property and earnings belonging to their husbands, their children under their husbands' control, their bodies their husbands' property. The Enlightenment changed nothing about women's legal status. If anything, it entrenched that status further by providing new "rational" justifications for it.

THE DEVIL thus fulfilled his role in the Enlightenment by building philosophical frameworks that justified women's exclusion (the theories of Rousseau, Kant, and others), codifying that exclusion in new legal systems (the Napoleonic Code and constitutional arrangements), and ensuring that the new freedoms being won for "humanity" were actually freedoms for men alone.

· · ·

Evidence for the Prosecution: MAN

Individual men—philosophers, legislators, husbands, fathers—enacted and enforced the Enlightenment's exclusion of women. They wrote the treatises that declared women's inferiority. They drafted the constitutions that denied women citizenship. They voted in the assemblies that excluded women from political participation. They enforced in their households the subordination that philosophy justified and law mandated.

The Male Monopoly on "Universal" Discourse

The Enlightenment was a conversation among men. The great philosophers corresponded with each other, debated with each other, responded to each other's works. Women were almost entirely excluded from this discourse. They couldn't attend universities, couldn't join learned societies, couldn't publish in the same venues, couldn't participate as equals in intellectual life.

Some women created spaces for intellectual engagement—the salons of Paris, for example, where educated women hosted gatherings of philosophers and writers. But even in these spaces, women were hosts and facilitators, not primary participants. They provided the venue for male genius to flourish; they were not themselves considered geniuses.

Women who did participate in Enlightenment discourse did so despite enormous obstacles. Émilie du Châtelet (1706-1749) was a brilliant mathematician and physicist who translated Newton's *Principia* into French and wrote important works on physics and philosophy. She was Voltaire's intellectual partner and in many ways his superior in mathematical reasoning. Yet she is barely remembered while Voltaire is celebrated as a towering Enlightenment figure.

The few women who gained recognition often had to disguise their sex or minimize their femininity to be taken seriously. And even then, male philosophers like Kant suggested that intellectual women might as well "grow a beard"—that intellectual achievement was fundamentally incompatible with femininity.

Men thus controlled the discourse that determined who counted as human, who deserved rights, who possessed reason. They defined reason in ways that excluded women. They defined humanity in ways that subordinated women. And they did all this while claiming to speak universal truths about human nature.

The Silencing of Female Voices

When women did speak up, men silenced them. The most dramatic example is Olympe de Gouges (1748-1793), who in 1791 published the *Declaration of the Rights of Woman and of the Female Citizen*, modeled on the revolutionary Declaration of the Rights of Man. She demanded that "woman is born free and remains equal to man in rights" and that "the principle of all sovereignty rests essentially in the nation, which is but the reuniting of woman and man."

De Gouges was executed by guillotine in 1793—not specifically for her feminist writings, but her challenge to male power certainly contributed to her fate. The prosecutor reportedly declared that she had "forgotten the virtues which belong to her sex."

Mary Wollstonecraft (1759-1797) published *A Vindication of the Rights of Woman* in 1792, directly challenging Rousseau's views on female education. She argued that women appeared inferior only because they were denied education, that reason was not gendered, that women deserved the same intellectual development as men.

Wollstonecraft was taken somewhat seriously during her lifetime, but after her death, when her husband published a memoir revealing her unconventional personal life (affairs, an illegitimate child, suicide attempts), she was savagely attacked. Her ideas were dismissed because of her "immorality." For nearly a century after her death, respectable women avoided mentioning her name. The message was clear: women who challenged male authority would be destroyed.

The Enlightenment Household

In the Enlightenment home, men exercised the same authority their fathers and grandfathers had exercised. They controlled family property. They made decisions about their children's education and marriages. They expected wifely obedience and domestic service. Philosophy might teach that all men were equal, but within the household, the husband was lord and the wife was servant.

Even the most enlightened philosophers lived this way. Rousseau, who wrote so eloquently about natural equality and the corrupting influence of civilization, abandoned his five children to foundling hospitals rather than raise them. He demanded from his common-law wife Thérèse Levasseur exactly the submission and service he prescribed for all women in his philosophy.

Kant, who never married, was served by a succession of housekeepers whose labor freed him to pursue his philosophical work. The great philosopher of human dignity and rational autonomy depended on women's unpaid domestic labor to sustain his intellectual production—labor that, according to his own philosophy, women were naturally suited to provide.

MAN thus fulfilled his role in the Enlightenment's exclusion of women by controlling intellectual discourse (defining reason in ways that excluded women), silencing women who challenged male authority (destroying de Gouges and Wollstonecraft), and enforcing domestic subordination (maintaining household authority regardless of philosophical principles).

• • •

The Voice in the Wilderness: Mary Wollstonecraft

In 1792, Mary Wollstonecraft published *A Vindication of the Rights of Woman*. This remarkable work exposed the Enlightenment's hypocrisy and demanded that its principles be extended to women.

Wollstonecraft's argument was straightforward: if reason is what distinguishes humans from animals, and if virtue depends on the exercise of reason, and if women are human beings with souls capable of salvation, then women must be educated to develop their reason just as men are. To deny women rational education is to deny their humanity.

She directly attacked Rousseau's program for female education:

"Women are told from their infancy, and taught by the example of their mothers, that a little knowledge of human weakness, justly termed cunning, softness of temper, outward obedience, and a scrupulous attention to a puerile kind of propriety, will obtain for them the protection of man."

Women weren't naturally inferior, Wollstonecraft argued. They were *made* inferior by the education they received—an education designed to make them pleasing to men rather than capable of independent thought. The apparent intellectual differences between men and women were the product of training, not nature.

This was a devastating argument. The Enlightenment's own principles—the blank slate, the primacy of reason, the importance of education—all supported women's equality. If Locke was right that the mind was a blank slate shaped by experience, then women's apparent inferiority resulted from their inferior experience (education), not their inferior nature. If Kant was right that rational beings deserved autonomy and respect, then women deserved autonomy and respect. If Rousseau was right that civilization corrupted natural equality, then the subordination of women was a corruption, not a natural state.

Wollstonecraft turned the Enlightenment's arguments against itself. She accepted the premises—reason, education, natural rights—and showed that they led inevitably to women's equality. The philosophers who excluded women weren't applying universal principles consistently; they were carving out an exception for half of humanity because they wanted to maintain their power.

But Wollstonecraft was largely ignored, then vilified. Her arguments were not refuted; they were dismissed because of her gender and her personal life. It would take more than a century before her ideas gained serious traction, and even then, the battle for women's equality would be long and brutal.

• • •

The Enlightenment's Legacy

The Enlightenment's exclusion of women was not an unfortunate blind spot that subsequent generations easily corrected. It was a deliberate theoretical position, defended by the era's greatest minds, encoded in new legal systems, and enforced by individual men in their households and institutions. Overcoming this exclusion would require centuries of struggle.

In some ways, the Enlightenment made women's subordination harder to challenge. Medieval theology could be criticized on religious grounds—other interpretations of Scripture, other theological traditions, other revelations. But "Nature" and "Reason" seemed to brook no argument. If science and philosophy proved that women were naturally inferior, what could be said against it?

The Enlightenment also created new forms of exclusion. In kingdoms and empires, aristocratic women sometimes wielded significant power—as queens, regents, influential noblewomen. The new democracies that emerged from Enlightenment thought excluded women entirely from political participation. Maria Theresa could rule the Habsburg Empire; no woman could vote in the French Republic or the United States.

The Enlightenment's great achievement was to establish the principles of human liberty, equality, and rights. Its great failure was to define "human" in a way that excluded women. The principles themselves would eventually be extended to women—but only after enormous struggle, and always over the resistance of men who argued that the Enlightenment never intended to include women.

The Masculine Triad had adapted successfully to a new intellectual era. Where medieval subordination rested on divine authority, Enlightenment subordination rested on "rational" claims about natural differences. Where the Church had declared women spiritually inferior, philosophers declared them rationally inferior. Where kings and priests had governed women through force and tradition, the new democratic order would govern them through law and philosophy.

The forms changed. The substance remained. Women were subordinate—not because God commanded it, but because Nature designed it. Not because Eve sinned, but because female brains were built differently. Not because tradition required it, but because scientific reason proved it.

And men—individual men, with names and faces and choices—created these systems, defended these philosophies, wrote these laws, and enforced this subordination in their homes. The Enlightenment was their project, conducted in their languages, published in their journals, debated in their academies. Women were objects of study, not participants in inquiry. They were topics of philosophy, not philosophers.

The age that proclaimed human liberation excluded half of humanity from its liberation. The movement that championed reason defined reason as male. The revolution that toppled kings enthroned husbands.

This was the Enlightenment's great betrayal: not that it failed to immediately achieve women's equality, but that it theorized and justified women's exclusion with all the intellectual sophistication at its command. The Masculine Triad had new weapons now—scientific authority, philosophical argument, constitutional law. And it would use them to maintain its power for centuries to come.

CHAPTER NINE

Rousseau and the Natural Woman

Jean-Jacques Rousseau (1712-1778) was perhaps the most influential philosopher of his age. His ideas shaped the French Revolution, inspired democratic movements across Europe and the Americas, and fundamentally transformed Western thought about freedom, education, and the relationship between individuals and society. He proclaimed that humans are born free and good, that civilization corrupts natural virtue, that legitimate government requires the consent of the governed, and that the "general will" of the people should determine the laws they live under.

He also created the most comprehensive, sophisticated, and influential philosophical justification for female subordination in modern history.

Rousseau deserves special attention because he was not merely a philosopher who happened to hold sexist views—a product of his time who didn't extend his progressive ideas to women. He was a philosopher who deliberately, systematically, and at great length argued that women *must* be subordinated to men, that this subordination was natural, necessary, and beneficial, and that any attempt to educate women for equality would be disastrous for civilization.

Where other Enlightenment philosophers treated women's exclusion as an afterthought or an unexamined assumption, Rousseau made it central to his project. His treatise *Emile, or On Education* (1762), which he called "the best and most important of all my writings," devoted its entire final book to explaining why women must be educated for subordination. His political philosophy in *The Social Contract* explicitly excluded women from citizenship. His vision of the ideal society depended fundamentally on women being confined to the domestic sphere and subject to male authority.

Rousseau matters because his ideas worked. They shaped educational practices, legal codes, and social expectations for centuries. The "cult of domesticity" that confined middle-class women to the home in the nineteenth century drew directly from Rousseau. The "separate spheres" ideology that excluded women from public life cited Rousseau as its philosophical foundation. The arguments against women's education, women's suffrage, and women's equality repeated Rousseau's claims about natural differences between the sexes.

To understand how the Masculine Triad adapted to the modern era, we must understand Rousseau. He provided the template.

• • •

The Paradox of Rousseau

Before examining Rousseau's views on women, we must appreciate the apparent contradiction they represent. This was a man who championed human freedom and equality. His *Discourse on the Origin of Inequality* (1755) argued that inequality was not natural but artificial—the product of corrupt civilization rather than inherent human nature. His *Social Contract* (1762) began with the famous declaration: "Man is born free, and everywhere he is in chains."

Rousseau attacked the divine right of kings, challenged hereditary aristocracy, and proclaimed that legitimate government could only rest on the consent of the governed. He rejected the idea that some people were naturally suited to rule and others to be ruled. He insisted that the authority of one person over another must be justified by something other than force or tradition.

All of these revolutionary ideas stopped at the threshold of gender.

Rousseau argued that while men were born free and should not be subject to arbitrary authority, women were born for subordination. While class distinctions were artificial corruptions, sex distinctions were natural and must be maintained. While men should be educated for autonomy and citizenship, women should be educated for obedience and domesticity. While men should participate in the "general will" that governed society, women should submit to male authority in the home.

This was not an inconsistency that Rousseau failed to notice. He directly addressed it. He argued that the subordination of women was different from other forms of hierarchy because it was *natural*—built into the very structure of sex differences—rather than artificial. The subjection of the poor to the rich was unjust because it resulted from corrupt social arrangements. The subjection of women to men was just because it resulted from nature itself.

The Masculine Triad had found its modern philosopher. Where medieval theology had grounded female subordination in divine command, Rousseau grounded it in natural necessity. Where the

Church had appealed to Scripture, Rousseau appealed to science. Where tradition had relied on custom and authority, Rousseau relied on reason and observation.

The conclusions were identical. Only the justifications had changed.

• • •

Evidence for the Prosecution: GOD

Rousseau's "God" was Nature. He rejected the authority of organized religion and the Church, but he replaced divine command with natural order. And Nature, as Rousseau interpreted it, had designed women for subordination just as surely as the God of Genesis had.

Nature's Design for Sexual Difference

In Book V of *Emile*, Rousseau begins his discussion of women's education by establishing their natural differences from men:

> *"In everything not connected with sex, woman is man.*
> *She has the same organs, the same needs, the same*
> *faculties... In everything connected with sex, woman and*
> *man are in every respect related and in every respect*
> *different."*

This might sound egalitarian—in everything not connected with sex, woman is man's equal. But Rousseau's point is that sex pervades *everything*. Sexual difference is not confined to reproductive organs; it shapes character, intellect, morality, and social role. For Rousseau, there is nothing about women that is not connected to sex.

The male is "active and strong," the female "passive and weak." This difference, Rousseau argues, is not merely physical but psychological and moral. Men are naturally suited for action, reason, and public life. Women are naturally suited for passivity, feeling, and domestic life. These are not social constructs but natural facts, as immutable as the difference between male and female bodies.

Nature has designed women to please and to serve men:

> *"The whole education of women ought to be relative to men. To please them, to be useful to them, to make themselves loved and honored by them, to educate them when young, to care for them when grown, to counsel them, to console them, and to make life agreeable and sweet to them—these are the duties of women at all times, and should be taught them from their infancy."*

Note the totality of this claim. Women's *whole* education—not part of it, not one aspect among many, but everything—should be relative to men. Women do not exist for themselves. They exist for men. Their purpose is to please, serve, comfort, and support the men in their lives. This is not a social expectation that might be changed; it is a natural duty that must be fulfilled.

The Natural Virtue of Modesty

Rousseau argues that Nature has given women modesty as a necessary check on sexual impulses. If women were as sexually aggressive as men, the result would be chaos—"the destruction of both sexes and the human race would perish through the very means established for preserving it."

Therefore, Nature has wisely made women modest, reserved, and defensive about sexual advances. Women must appear reluctant even when willing; they must say no even when they mean yes; they must guard their reputation above all else. This is not social convention but natural necessity.

This argument has devastating implications. If women are naturally designed to refuse sexual advances while secretly welcoming them, then a woman's "no" is meaningless. If women must preserve their reputations by appearing reluctant, then apparent reluctance is not genuine reluctance. Rousseau has provided a philosophical justification for ignoring women's stated wishes about their own bodies.

Moreover, Rousseau argues that women must care primarily about reputation—about what others think of them—rather than about actual virtue. For men, "opinion is the grave of virtue." For women, opinion "is its throne." A man should do what is right regardless of others' opinions. A woman should do what appears right to others, regardless of what is actually right.

This strips women of moral autonomy. A man is a moral agent who determines right and wrong through his own reason. A woman is a social performer who determines right and wrong based on what others will think. She has no independent moral standing; her virtue is entirely dependent on others' perceptions.

The Religion of Domesticity

Rousseau creates what amounts to a secular religion of domesticity. The home becomes the sacred space where women fulfill their natural destiny. Motherhood becomes the highest calling, not a choice but a duty commanded by Nature. The division between public (male) and private (female) spheres becomes as absolute as the division between sacred and profane.

Women who violate this natural order—who seek education, public roles, or independence from male authority—are not merely unconventional. They are unnatural. They have transgressed against Nature's design as surely as a heretic transgresses against God's law.

Rousseau's Nature thus fulfills GOD's role in the Masculine Triad by providing ultimate authority for female subordination (natural necessity rather than divine command), establishing sexual difference as all-encompassing (affecting every aspect of character and capacity), stripping women of moral autonomy (making their virtue dependent on others' opinions rather than their own reason), and sacralizing domesticity (making the home a temple and motherhood a religious vocation).

. . .

Evidence for the Prosecution: THE DEVIL

If Nature provided the justification, Rousseau's philosophy provided the practical program for subordinating women. His detailed prescriptions for female education, his exclusion of women from citizenship, and his influence on subsequent legal and educational systems constitute the Devil's work in a new idiom.

The Education of Sophie: A Blueprint for Subordination

In *Emile*, Rousseau describes two educations: one for Emile, a boy being raised to become a free, rational, autonomous citizen; and one for Sophie, a girl being raised to become Emile's wife. The contrast is systematic and total.

Emile's education develops his natural faculties. He learns through experience and exploration. He is encouraged to question, investigate, and reason for himself. He is protected from social corruption so that his natural goodness can flourish. He is educated to be independent, self-governing, and capable of participating in civic life.

Sophie's education does exactly the opposite. She learns to please others rather than develop herself. She is taught constraint, not exploration. She is encouraged to accept authority rather than question it. She is trained for dependency, not independence. She is educated to serve men, not to govern herself.

Rousseau is explicit about this difference:

"To cultivate masculine virtues in women and to neglect their own is evidently to do them injury... When women try to usurp our privileges they do not abandon their own; with this result: they are unable to make use of two incompatible things, so they fall below their own level as women, instead of rising to the level of man."

A woman who seeks masculine virtues—reason, independence, public achievement—destroys her feminine virtues without gaining masculine ones. She becomes nothing, a failed woman who can never be a real man. The only path to female excellence is through feminine subordination.

Sophie learns domestic skills—cooking, sewing, housekeeping. She learns social graces—conversation, music, charm. She learns to manage her appearance and reputation. She does *not* learn serious intellectual subjects. She does *not* learn to reason abstractly. She does *not* learn to think independently.

Rousseau argues that women are capable of practical intelligence but not theoretical reason. They can manage a household but not govern a state. They can please and charm but not discover truth. Intellectual development in women is not only unnecessary but harmful—it destroys the feminine charm that is their only source of power.

Exclusion from Citizenship

Rousseau's *Social Contract* establishes that legitimate government rests on the consent of the governed, expressed through the "general will." Citizens come together to form laws that bind everyone equally. This is the foundation of republican liberty.

But women are not citizens. They are not part of the general will. They do not participate in lawmaking. They are subject to laws they have no voice in creating.

As the Stanford Encyclopedia of Philosophy notes: "Rousseau's commitment to the freedom and equality of citizens is marred and limited to the fact that he envisages those citizens as exclusively male: women are subject to the authority of the state but have no voice in the determination of the general will."

This is not oversight or incomplete application of universal principles. It is deliberate exclusion based on Rousseau's conviction that women are not capable of the rational deliberation that citizenship requires. The social contract is a contract among men about how to govern everyone, including women. Women are governed but do not govern.

Moreover, Rousseau links citizenship to family structure. The good citizen is produced by the good family, and the good family requires female subordination. If women were citizens—if they had public roles and independent political voices—the family structure that produces good citizens would collapse. Female subordination is not just compatible with republican liberty; it is necessary for it.

The Lasting Legal and Educational Impact

Rousseau's ideas had enormous practical impact. His educational theories influenced pedagogical practice across Europe. His political philosophy shaped revolutionary movements and constitutional designs. His vision of domestic femininity became the template for middle-class womanhood.

The Napoleonic Code, which governed France and much of Europe, reflected Rousseauian assumptions about women's proper place. Women were legal subordinates of their husbands. They could not work, own property, or make contracts without male permission. They were excluded from public life and confined to the domestic sphere Rousseau had prescribed.

Educational systems across Europe and America followed Rousseau's prescriptions for sex-differentiated education. Girls learned domestic skills and social graces. Boys learned academic subjects and practical trades. The purpose of female education was to prepare women for their roles as wives and mothers, not to develop their intellectual capacities or prepare them for public life.

These patterns persisted well into the twentieth century. The "separate spheres" ideology, the "cult of domesticity," the resistance to women's education and suffrage—all of these drew on Rousseauian arguments about natural sexual difference and the proper roles of men and women.

THE DEVIL thus fulfilled his role through Rousseau by creating a comprehensive educational program for female subordination (the education of Sophie), providing philosophical justification for excluding women from citizenship (the gendered social contract), and influencing legal and educational systems across Europe and America (the Napoleonic Code and sex-differentiated schooling).

• • •

Evidence for the Prosecution: MAN

Rousseau was a man, and his philosophy served men's interests. But his personal life reveals the particular forms of male domination that his philosophy justified. The philosopher of female subordination practiced what he preached—and his practice reveals the human cost of his theories.

Rousseau's Personal Contradictions

Rousseau lived with Thérèse Levasseur, a semi-literate servant, for most of his adult life. She bore him five children. He abandoned all five to foundling homes, where most children died in infancy.

The philosopher who wrote so eloquently about natural education and maternal love refused to raise his own children. The man who argued that women should devote themselves to motherhood as their highest calling prevented his own partner from being a mother. The thinker who celebrated the family as the foundation of civic virtue destroyed his own family before it could begin.

Rousseau's justifications were revealing. He claimed he couldn't afford to raise children. He claimed Thérèse's family would corrupt them. He claimed it was better for the children to be raised by the state than by their actual parents.

But the deeper truth is that children would have interfered with Rousseau's work. Raising five children would have required time, money, and attention that Rousseau preferred to spend on his writing. The philosopher of natural domesticity abandoned his domestic responsibilities so that he could write about how important domestic responsibilities were for women.

This is the Masculine Triad in miniature. Rousseau theorized that women should sacrifice themselves for their families while he himself sacrificed his family for his career. He argued that women's highest purpose was motherhood while preventing Thérèse from being a mother. He praised domestic virtue while practicing domestic abandonment.

The Subordination of Thérèse

Thérèse Levasseur was exactly the kind of woman Rousseau's philosophy prescribed—uneducated, domestic, devoted to her man. She could barely read. She had no intellectual interests. She served Rousseau's needs without making demands of her own.

And Rousseau treated her accordingly. He never married her until late in life, and then only in an informal ceremony. He frequently expressed embarrassment about her in intellectual company. He took her services for granted while condescending to her limitations— limitations his own philosophy insisted were natural and proper for women.

Thérèse had no power in the relationship. She couldn't prevent Rousseau from abandoning their children. She couldn't demand education or intellectual engagement. She couldn't claim public recognition as Rousseau's partner. She lived the subordination that

Rousseau prescribed for all women—and her life demonstrated its costs.

The Male Audience for Male Philosophy

Rousseau wrote for men. His educational treatises were addressed to fathers and tutors. His political philosophy assumed male citizens deliberating about the common good. His vision of the ideal society was a vision of male flourishing supported by female service.

Women appear in Rousseau's work as objects to be educated, managed, and enjoyed—not as subjects with their own perspectives and interests. Sophie exists for Emile. Female citizens (if the term even applies) exist to support male citizenship. Mothers exist to raise sons who will be citizens and daughters who will raise more sons.

Male readers found in Rousseau a flattering portrait of themselves as naturally superior, rational, and suited for public life. They found justification for their authority over women. They found a philosophical framework that made their dominance seem natural and necessary rather than arbitrary and unjust.

Rousseau told men what they wanted to hear: that their power over women was not a historical accident or a social construction but a natural necessity. That women who challenged male authority were not seeking justice but violating nature. That the subordination of women was not oppression but the fulfillment of women's own nature.

MAN thus fulfilled his role in Rousseau's system by writing philosophy that served male interests (justifying male authority as natural), practicing domestic subordination (his treatment of Thérèse and their children), and creating a male audience for theories of female inferiority (philosophers, educators, and legislators who implemented Rousseau's vision).

• • •

The Wollstonecraft Response

Mary Wollstonecraft recognized what Rousseau had done. In *A Vindication of the Rights of Woman* (1792), she systematically dismantled his arguments about female nature and education.

Wollstonecraft accepted Rousseau's premise that reason was what distinguished humans from animals and made them capable of virtue. But she drew the opposite conclusion: if reason is the human faculty, and if virtue depends on reason, then women—who are human—must be educated to develop their reason, not trained to suppress it.

She attacked Rousseau's claim that women should care about reputation rather than actual virtue:

"Women are told from their infancy, and taught by the example of their mothers, that a little knowledge of human weakness, justly termed cunning, softness of temper, outward obedience, and a scrupulous attention to a puerile kind of propriety, will obtain for them the protection of man."

This education in dependency and deception, Wollstonecraft argued, made women exactly what Rousseau claimed they naturally were—weak, vain, cunning, concerned only with appearance. But this was the product of education, not nature. Give women the same education as men and they would demonstrate the same capacities.

Wollstonecraft pointed out the devastating circularity of Rousseau's argument: deny women education, then cite their apparent intellectual inferiority as proof that they don't deserve education. Train women for subordination, then cite their subordinate behavior as proof that subordination is natural. Create the very conditions that produce female "weakness," then claim that weakness is inherent.

She also noted Rousseau's inconsistency. His philosophy proclaimed that humans were naturally good but corrupted by civilization. If this was true of men, why not of women? If men's apparent vices were products of corrupt social arrangements rather than natural depravity, why should women's apparent limitations be attributed to nature rather than society?

But Wollstonecraft's response, powerful as it was, could not undo Rousseau's influence. Her book was controversial and her reputation was destroyed after her death. Rousseau remained the dominant voice on education and women's nature for generations. The Masculine Triad had found its philosopher, and his ideas would shape Western thought—and Western women's lives—for centuries to come.

• • •

Rousseau's Legacy

Rousseau died in 1778. His ideas lived on, shaping the French Revolution (whose leaders idolized him), the Napoleonic Code (which implemented his vision of female subordination), educational reform movements (which followed his prescriptions for sex-differentiated education), and domestic ideology (which enshrined his "separate spheres" as natural and proper).

The nineteenth century's "cult of domesticity" was Rousseauian through and through. Women were told that their proper sphere was the home, that their highest calling was motherhood, that intellectual pursuits would destroy their feminine nature. They were educated for domesticity, excluded from higher education and the professions, denied political rights, and confined to the private sphere that Rousseau had prescribed.

When women began demanding rights—education, property, suffrage—the arguments against them echoed Rousseau. Women were naturally different from men. Their nature suited them for private rather than public life. Equality would destroy femininity and with it the family, the foundation of civilization. These were Rousseau's arguments, repeated by legislators, educators, clergy, and ordinary men who wanted to maintain their authority.

Rousseau's influence persists today. The idea that women are "naturally" more nurturing, emotional, and suited for caregiving—while men are "naturally" more rational, aggressive, and suited for leadership —draws on Rousseauian assumptions about sexual difference. The expectation that women will sacrifice career ambitions for family responsibilities reflects Rousseau's vision of female destiny. The double standards around sexuality—women who are sexually active judged more harshly than men—echo Rousseau's claims about female modesty and reputation.

The Masculine Triad has had few more effective servants than Jean-Jacques Rousseau. He provided what the Triad needed to survive the Enlightenment: a philosophical justification for female subordination that didn't rely on divine authority or naked tradition, that appealed to reason and nature, that seemed progressive and modern while preserving the oldest of hierarchies.

God had commanded women to submit. Now Nature commanded it. The chains remained. Only the lock had changed.

CHAPTER TEN

The French Revolution's Betrayal

On August 26, 1789, the National Constituent Assembly of France adopted the Declaration of the Rights of Man and of the Citizen. This document, born of revolution and inspired by Enlightenment philosophy, proclaimed that "men are born and remain free and equal in rights." It declared that the purpose of government was to preserve the natural and imprescriptible rights of man: liberty, property, security, and resistance to oppression. It established that law was the expression of the general will and that every citizen had the right to participate in its formation.

It was a document that would inspire democratic movements across the globe for centuries to come. It was also, from its very first word, a lie.

The word "man" in the Declaration of the Rights of Man was not a generic term for humanity. It meant men specifically—male human beings. The revolutionary leaders who drafted this document, who stormed the Bastille in the name of liberty and overthrew a king in the name of equality, never intended for their lofty principles to apply to women. They proclaimed universal rights while excluding half of humanity from those rights. They declared all men equal while maintaining that women were naturally subordinate. They overthrew one form of tyranny while preserving another.

The French Revolution represents the most dramatic betrayal in the history of women's struggle for freedom. It was not simply that revolutionaries failed to extend rights to women—an oversight that might be attributed to the limitations of their time. It was that they actively, deliberately, and violently suppressed women's demands for inclusion. They debated women's rights and rejected them. They heard women's petitions and ignored them. They watched women fight for the revolution and then excluded them from its benefits. And when women persisted in demanding equality, they executed them.

To understand how the Masculine Triad operates, we must understand the French Revolution. Here was a moment when the old order collapsed, when everything seemed possible, when the chains of tradition and authority appeared to be breaking. And in that moment of maximum possibility, men chose to preserve their power over women. They chose to build a new order on the same ancient foundation of female subordination.

Liberty, Equality, Fraternity—for men only.

• • •

The Promise: Women in the Revolutionary Moment

Women were not passive observers of the French Revolution. They were participants, activists, and in many ways the driving force behind some of its most decisive moments.

The Women's March on Versailles

On October 5, 1789, the women of Paris launched one of the Revolution's most consequential actions. Driven by hunger—bread was scarce and expensive—and by revolutionary fervor, thousands of market women marched from Paris to Versailles, a distance of about twelve miles. They carried makeshift weapons: pikes, pitchforks, kitchen knives, even a cannon. Along the way, their numbers swelled as more women joined them.

When they reached Versailles, they invaded the National Assembly, demanding bread and demanding that the king acknowledge the revolutionary changes. The next morning, a crowd broke into the palace itself, and two of the queen's guards were killed. The women forced the royal family to return to Paris with them, effectively ending the king's ability to resist the Revolution from his isolated palace.

This was not a bread riot. It was a political action that fundamentally altered the course of the Revolution. The women of Paris had done what the men of the National Assembly could not: they had brought the king to heel. They had demonstrated that the people— including the female people—had power.

Yet when the Declaration of the Rights of Man was finalized just weeks earlier, women were not mentioned. When the National Assembly debated who should have political rights, women were explicitly excluded. The women who had made the Revolution possible were denied the Revolution's benefits.

Women's Political Activism

Throughout the revolutionary period, women organized, agitated, and demanded inclusion. They formed political clubs where they debated the issues of the day. They attended sessions of the National Assembly, the Jacobin Club, and the Cordeliers, though usually only as spectators who could not vote or speak. They wrote pamphlets, published newspapers, and circulated petitions.

The Société Fraternelle de Patriotes de Deux Sexes (Fraternal Society of Patriots of Both Sexes) admitted both men and women as members. The Amis de la Loi (Friends of the Law), founded by the revolutionary activist Théroigne de Méricourt, welcomed women's participation. Women like Etta Palm d'Aelders organized specifically to advocate for women's political rights, presenting petitions to the Assembly demanding equality.

In May 1793, Pauline Léon and Claire Lacombe founded the Society of Revolutionary Republican Women (Société des Citoyennes Républicaines Révolutionnaires), the most radical and visible women's political organization of the Revolution. With approximately 170 members, they met at the Jacobin library, wore the red cap of liberty, and demanded vigorous action against the Revolution's enemies. They called for women to be allowed to bear arms in defense of the Republic.

These women were not asking for special treatment. They were asking to be included in the rights that the Revolution claimed were universal and natural. They were asking for the Declaration of the Rights of Man to mean what it said.

The answer was no.

• • •

Evidence for the Prosecution: GOD

The French Revolution rejected the authority of the Catholic Church. It seized Church property, abolished religious orders, and eventually attempted to replace Christianity with a "Cult of Reason" and later a "Cult of the Supreme Being." The revolutionaries did not look to God for justification of their new order.

But they found a substitute god in Nature. And Nature, as interpreted by the revolutionary men, commanded female subordination just as surely as the God of Genesis had.

The Ideology of Natural Difference

Rousseau's philosophy pervaded revolutionary thought. His Social Contract provided the theoretical foundation for popular sovereignty. His concept of the "general will" shaped how revolutionaries understood democratic participation. And his views on women—that they were naturally different from men, naturally suited for domesticity, naturally subordinate—shaped how revolutionaries understood citizenship.

When the National Assembly debated who should be included in the category of "active citizens" with political rights, they drew on Rousseauian assumptions about natural sexual difference. Men were rational, independent, capable of participating in the general will. Women were emotional, dependent, suited only for the private sphere of home and family.

This was presented not as prejudice but as science. The revolutionaries believed they were following nature's design, not merely preserving old customs. They were creating a rational society based on natural principles—and those natural principles happened to require female subordination.

The Sacralization of Motherhood

Revolutionary ideology created a new religion of republican motherhood. Women were told that their contribution to the nation would be through bearing and raising virtuous citizens—male citizens who would participate in public life while their mothers remained in the domestic sphere.

This was framed as an honor rather than an exclusion. Women were elevated as mothers of the republic, guardians of private virtue, the foundation upon which public virtue rested. But the elevation was a cage. Women were praised for their essential contribution while being denied any role in defining what that contribution should be.

The revolutionary festivals that celebrated the new order made this ideology visible. Allegorical female figures represented Liberty, Reason, and the Republic—but actual women were largely excluded from political participation. Women could be symbols of freedom; they could not exercise it.

The Doctrine of Separate Spheres

Revolutionary ideology hardened the distinction between public and private spheres that Rousseau had advocated. The public sphere—politics, commerce, intellectual life—belonged to men. The private sphere—home, family, domestic management—belonged to women. These were not arbitrary social arrangements but natural necessities, built into the very structure of sexual difference.

Men who crossed into the domestic sphere were merely helping their wives. Women who crossed into the public sphere were unnatural, dangerous, threatening to the social order. The separate spheres doctrine made female subordination seem not like oppression but like the natural order of things—a fulfillment of women's nature rather than a violation of their rights.

GOD thus fulfilled his role in the revolutionary Masculine Triad by replacing divine command with natural necessity (Nature commanded what the Church once commanded), sacralizing motherhood and domesticity (making women's confinement seem like elevation), and providing ideological justification for excluding women from citizenship (separate spheres as natural rather than artificial).

• • •

Evidence for the Prosecution: THE DEVIL

The revolutionary men did not merely fail to include women in their new order. They actively, deliberately, and systematically excluded them—through law, through policy, and ultimately through violence.

The Declaration of the Rights of Man: Exclusion by Design

The Declaration of the Rights of Man and of the Citizen, adopted August 26, 1789, was drafted primarily by the Marquis de Lafayette with input from Thomas Jefferson and finalized by Abbé Sieyès and others. Its language appears universal: "Men are born and remain free and equal in rights." But the Constitution of 1791, which the Declaration preceded, made clear that "men" meant men.

The Constitution distinguished between "active citizens" and "passive citizens." Active citizens—those with political rights including voting—were defined as men who were French, at least 25 years old, paid taxes equal to three days' work, and were not servants. Passive citizens were everyone else: the poor, servants, foreigners, and all women regardless of wealth or status.

Women were explicitly categorized with children, the mentally incompetent, and criminals—persons incapable of rational political participation. The revolutionary leaders debated this exclusion; they did not stumble into it by accident. The Marquis de Condorcet argued that the same logic that justified rights for men justified rights for women, but his arguments were rejected. The exclusion of women was a conscious choice.

In November 1789, shortly after the Women's March on Versailles, a group of women submitted a petition to the National Assembly requesting the extension of equality to women. Like thousands of other petitions, it was never discussed. The Assembly that would debate for hours about the rights of Jews, Protestants, free Blacks, and propertyless men refused even to consider the rights of women.

The Suppression of Women's Political Activity

As the Revolution radicalized, women's political activism intensified—and so did the backlash against it. By 1793, the most radical phase of the Revolution, women were demanding not just inclusion but armed participation in the defense of the Republic. The Society of Revolutionary Republican Women called for women to bear arms against internal enemies. They demanded vigorous enforcement of price controls to make bread affordable. They wore the red cap of liberty and the tricolor cockade as signs of their revolutionary commitment.

On October 29, 1793, a group of market women appeared before the National Convention to complain that members of the Society of Revolutionary Republican Women had tried to force them to wear the revolutionary cockade. This provided the occasion for a broader discussion of women's political activity.

The next day, October 30, 1793, Jean-Baptiste Amar spoke for the Committee of Public Security and proposed a decree suppressing all women's political clubs. His speech laid out the revolutionary government's official position on women:

> *"Should women exercise political rights and meddle in the affairs of government? In general, we can answer no. You will ask why? Because they would be obligated to sacrifice more important cares to which nature calls them. The private functions to which women are destined*

by nature itself follow from the general order of society. This social order results from the difference between man and woman. Each sex is called to a type of occupation that is proper to it... Man is strong, robust, born with great energy, audacity, and courage... Woman is constituted to be the companion of man."

The Convention passed the decree with virtually no discussion. All women's political clubs were banned. Women were ordered to return to their homes and tend to their families, leaving public affairs to men.

This was not a conservative reaction against the Revolution. This was the Jacobin government at the height of its radicalism, the same government that was executing aristocrats and suspected counter-revolutionaries by the thousands. The men who believed themselves history's most radical champions of liberty and equality deliberately excluded women from both.

The Execution of Olympe de Gouges

Marie Gouze, known as Olympe de Gouges (1748-1793), was a playwright, political activist, and pamphleteer who had supported the Revolution from its earliest days. She advocated for the abolition of slavery, divorce rights, and welfare for the poor. In September 1791, she published her most famous work: the Declaration of the Rights of Woman and of the Female Citizen.

De Gouges structured her declaration as a point-by-point parallel to the Declaration of the Rights of Man, demonstrating how each article should apply equally to women. Her most famous passage declared: "Woman has the right to mount the scaffold; she must equally have the right to mount the rostrum." If women could be executed for political crimes—if they were subject to the laws—then they must also have the right to participate in making those laws.

Her declaration was ignored by the National Assembly. But de Gouges continued writing and agitating, increasingly critical of the Revolution's violent turn. She opposed the execution of Louis XVI and attacked the radical Jacobin leader Robespierre. Her pamphlet "The Three Urns" (Les Trois Urnes) advocated for federalism and criticized the centralized revolutionary government.

In July 1793, de Gouges was arrested. She was charged with sedition and with being an enemy of the Republic. Her trial was a mockery—she was denied the right to a lawyer, with the judge declaring that her writings proved she was capable of defending herself. On November 3, 1793, she was executed by guillotine.

A report on her death made the political message explicit:

> *"Olympe de Gouges, born with an exalted imagination,*
> *mistook her delirium for an inspiration of nature. She*
> *wanted to be a man of state. She took up the projects of*
> *the perfidious people who want to divide France. It seems*
> *the law has punished this conspirator for having*
> *forgotten the virtues that belong to her sex."*

She was executed, in other words, not merely for her political opinions but for having political opinions at all. She had "forgotten the virtues that belong to her sex." She had tried to be a "man of state." Her crime was being a woman who participated in public life.

De Gouges was the only woman executed primarily for her political writings during the Revolution. Her death was a message to all women: this is what happens when you forget your place.

The Silencing Continues

After the banning of women's clubs in October 1793, the suppression of women's political activity accelerated. On November 17, 1793, the General Council of the Paris Commune adopted a proposal that no future female deputations would be received. Women could no longer even petition the government as a group.

In May 1795, the Convention went further, declaring that women would be kept out of the galleries altogether. They could no longer even observe the proceedings of the government that ruled them. Women had been reduced from citizens demanding rights to spectators observing from the galleries to persons barred even from watching.

Prominent female activists were punished for their militancy. Théroigne de Méricourt, who had organized women's political clubs and called for female military service, was arrested, publicly flogged by a mob of Jacobin women (who attacked her for allegedly supporting the Girondins), and spent the rest of her life in an asylum. Claire Lacombe, co-founder of the Society of Revolutionary Republican Women, was imprisoned. Pauline Léon was arrested and detained.

The message was clear: women who engaged in politics would be destroyed.

• • •

Evidence for the Prosecution: MAN

The revolutionary leaders were men, and they acted in men's interests. They created a new political order that preserved and enhanced male power while systematically excluding women from that power.

The Men Who Made the Revolution

The National Assembly, the Legislative Assembly, the National Convention, the Committee of Public Safety—every institution of revolutionary government was exclusively male. The men who debated the rights of man, who drafted constitutions, who decided questions of war and peace, who sent thousands to the guillotine—all of them were men.

Some of these men, like the Marquis de Condorcet, argued for women's inclusion. Condorcet published "On the Admission of Women to the Rights of Citizenship" in 1790, arguing that the same natural rights that justified political equality among men justified equality between men and women. He was ignored by his fellow revolutionaries—and he was later executed during the Terror, though for other reasons.

But most revolutionary men saw no contradiction between proclaiming universal rights and excluding women. Jean-Baptiste Amar could argue that nature destined women for private functions without anyone in the Convention objecting. Philippe Fabre d'Églantine could denounce women's clubs as unnatural without being challenged. The Jacobin leaders who sent thousands to the guillotine for insufficient revolutionary zeal never considered that excluding women might be counter-revolutionary.

Male Power Preserved

The Revolution abolished aristocratic privilege. It ended feudal obligations. It confiscated Church property. It executed the king. But it preserved male authority over women virtually intact.

Within marriage, husbands retained their traditional authority. Women gained some rights during the early revolutionary period—including the right to divorce, established in 1792—but these were limited and precarious. The fundamental structure of male headship of household remained.

In property law, some reforms benefited women. The egalitarian inheritance laws of 1791 gave daughters equal rights with sons to inherit family property. But married women's property remained under their husbands' control. And these gains would prove temporary—the Napoleonic Code would soon reverse most of them.

In education, revolutionary rhetoric celebrated the importance of educating women to be good republican mothers. But this education was designed to prepare women for domesticity, not for citizenship. Girls were not educated for independence or public life but for service to husbands and children.

The Brotherhood of Man

The revolutionary slogan was "Liberty, Equality, Fraternity"—and fraternity means brotherhood. The revolutionaries imagined themselves as brothers united against tyranny. This brotherhood was literal: it was a community of men.

Women could be mothers of citizens, wives of citizens, daughters of citizens—but not citizens themselves. They could support the brotherhood, serve the brotherhood, even sacrifice for the brotherhood —but they could not join it. The revolutionary community was a community of men, and women existed only in relation to the men to whom they were attached.

This brotherhood served men's collective interests. It created a public sphere from which women were excluded, where men could exercise power without female participation or oversight. It created a private sphere where men retained authority over women. It created a political system where men alone decided what rights women would have.

MAN thus fulfilled his role in the revolutionary Masculine Triad by monopolizing all revolutionary institutions (every legislative, executive, and judicial body was exclusively male), preserving male authority within the family (husbands remained heads of households), and creating a political brotherhood that excluded women (fraternity as literal male bonding).

• • •

The Final Betrayal: The Napoleonic Code

Whatever gains women had made during the revolutionary period were swept away by Napoleon Bonaparte. The Civil Code of 1804—the Napoleonic Code—consolidated and systematized female subordination in a way that would influence law across Europe and around the world for the next two centuries.

The Code's Provisions on Women

The Napoleonic Code established the supremacy of the husband over his wife and children. Its provisions regarding women read like a catalog of subjugation:

Article 213 stated: "The husband owes protection to his wife, the wife obedience to her husband." This was not reciprocal obligation but hierarchical command. The husband protected; the wife obeyed.

Article 214 required: "The wife is obliged to live with her husband, and to follow him to every place where he may judge it convenient to reside." A wife had no right to determine where she lived. Her husband decided, and she followed.

Article 215 specified: "The wife cannot plead in her own name, without the authority of her husband, even though she should be a public trader, or non-communicant, or separate in property." A woman could not go to court without her husband's permission. She could not sue or be sued, could not testify, could not participate in legal proceedings as an independent person.

Article 217 declared: "A wife, although non-communicant or separate in property, cannot give, alienate, pledge, or acquire by free or chargeable title, without the concurrence of her husband in the act, or his consent in writing." A woman could not buy, sell, give away, or receive property without her husband's permission. She could not enter into contracts. She had no independent economic existence.

The Code gave husbands control over all marital property, including any property a wife brought into the marriage. Husbands controlled their wives' earnings. Husbands determined how children would be raised and educated. Husbands could authorize or forbid their wives to work.

Divorce, which had been established in 1792, was still technically permitted but under conditions highly unfavorable to women. And in 1816, after Napoleon's fall, divorce was abolished altogether and would not be restored in France until 1884.

The Code's Influence

The Napoleonic Code was not merely French law. Napoleon imposed it throughout his empire, and it remained in force in many territories long after his defeat. Belgium, Luxembourg, parts of Germany, the Netherlands, Italy, Spain, and Poland all operated under the Code or codes heavily influenced by it. French colonies around the world were governed by its provisions.

Beyond Napoleon's direct rule, the Code became a model for legal modernization. Countries seeking to rationalize their legal systems often looked to the Napoleonic Code as a template. Its provisions on women—its systematic reduction of married women to legal subordinates—spread across continents.

The Code's influence persisted for generations. In France itself, married women did not gain the right to open bank accounts without their husbands' permission until 1965. They did not gain equal parental authority over children until 1970. The systematic subordination established in 1804 shaped women's lives well into the twentieth century.

Napoleon's Own Views

Napoleon personally oversaw the Code's development, chairing many of the commission's sessions. His views on women were unambiguous. He reportedly declared: "Women are nothing but machines for producing children." He believed women should be confined to domestic duties and excluded from public life.

The Code reflected Napoleon's personal misogyny, but it also reflected broader revolutionary ideology. The same men who had proclaimed liberty and equality, who had overthrown a king and executed aristocrats, created a legal system that reduced women to the status of perpetual minors. The Napoleonic Code was not a betrayal of revolutionary principles—it was their culmination with respect to women.

• • •

The Revolution's Legacy for Women

What did women gain from the French Revolution? In the short term, very little. Some reforms of the early revolutionary period—divorce rights, equal inheritance, civil marriage—were reversed or restricted. The legal status of women under the Napoleonic Code was in many ways worse than it had been under the old regime.

The Revolution did establish that rights could be claimed as natural and universal rather than as privileges granted by tradition or authority. This language of rights would eventually be turned against the revolutionaries' own exclusions. If rights were natural and universal, on what basis could women be denied them?

Olympe de Gouges had asked this question. Mary Wollstonecraft, writing in 1792, asked it as well. But their questions would not receive serious answers for another century and more. French women did not gain the right to vote until 1944—more than 150 years after the Revolution that had proclaimed liberty, equality, and fraternity.

The French Revolution demonstrates how the Masculine Triad operates in moments of crisis and transformation. When everything else changed—when monarchy fell, when aristocracy was abolished, when the Church lost its power—men's authority over women remained. It was the one constant in a world of revolutionary change.

This was not because women's subordination was too deeply rooted to challenge. The revolutionaries challenged far deeper-rooted institutions. It was because men chose to preserve their power over women. They made this choice deliberately, consciously, and violently. They debated women's rights and rejected them. They heard women's demands and silenced them. They created a new order and built it on the old foundation of female subjugation.

The revolution was not incomplete. It was not inconsistent. With respect to women, it achieved exactly what its male leaders intended: the preservation and strengthening of male power in a new ideological framework. The Masculine Triad had survived its greatest test and emerged stronger than before.

Liberty, Equality, Fraternity. But for women: Obedience, Domesticity, Silence.

CHAPTER ELEVEN

The Cult of Domesticity

In 1854, the English poet Coventry Patmore published the first installment of a long narrative poem that would become one of the most influential texts of the Victorian era. He called it "The Angel in the House." The poem celebrated his wife Emily as the embodiment of perfect womanhood: devoted, submissive, selfless, existing entirely to please her husband and create a moral sanctuary in the home.

> *Man must be pleased; but him to please*
> *Is woman's pleasure; down the gulf*
> *Of his condoled necessities*
> *She casts her best, she flings herself.*

This was not merely poetry. It was prescription. The "angel in the house" became the template for respectable womanhood across the English-speaking world and beyond. A woman's purpose was to please men. Her sphere was the home. Her virtues were submission, self-sacrifice, and silent devotion. She existed not for herself but for others— for her husband, her children, her household. She had no desires of her own, no ambitions beyond domestic perfection, no identity separate from her role as wife and mother.

Historians call this ideology the "cult of domesticity" or the "cult of true womanhood"—and "cult" is the appropriate word. It was a system of belief that demanded total commitment, punished deviation, and promised salvation through adherence to its strictures. The true woman was pious, pure, submissive, and domestic. Any woman who failed to embody these virtues was not merely unconventional; she was unnatural, unfeminine, dangerous to herself and to society.

The nineteenth century saw the cult of domesticity reach its apotheosis. It was the golden age of separate spheres, when the division between public and private life became absolute, when women's confinement to the home was elevated to sacred duty, and when the Masculine Triad perfected its modern form. God spoke through Nature and Science. The Devil worked through law, medicine, and social pressure. And Man exercised his authority with the confidence of one whose dominance was ordained by both theology and biology.

This chapter examines how the cult of domesticity operated to confine women, control their bodies, restrict their opportunities, and pathologize any attempt to escape the domestic cage. It is a story of ideology made material, of ideas that imprisoned.

• • •

The Four Cardinal Virtues

In 1966, historian Barbara Welter identified the four "cardinal virtues" that the cult of domesticity demanded of women: piety, purity, submissiveness, and domesticity. These were not merely desirable qualities; they were the defining characteristics of true womanhood. A woman who possessed them was virtuous. A woman who lacked them was fallen.

Piety

Religion was the one intellectual pursuit permitted to women—indeed, expected of them. Women were considered naturally more spiritual than men, closer to God, more attuned to moral and religious concerns. This was presented as a compliment, an acknowledgment of women's superiority in at least one realm.

But the compliment was a cage. Women's piety was to be exercised within the home, not in the public sphere. Women could not be ministers, could not preach, could not hold religious authority. Their role was to maintain the spiritual atmosphere of the household, to raise children in the faith, to provide a moral haven for husbands corrupted by the competitive world outside.

Moreover, the religion women were expected to practice was one of submission and self-abnegation. They were to model themselves on the suffering Christ, the passive Virgin. Female saints were celebrated for their martyrdom, their acceptance of suffering, their renunciation of worldly desires. Piety, for women, meant acceptance of their subordinate position as divinely ordained.

Purity

Sexual purity was the woman's "greatest treasure," the "pearl of great price" that she must guard above all else. A woman who lost her virginity before marriage was "ruined," "fallen," "lost"—the vocabulary itself reveals the ideology. Her entire value as a human being was located in her sexual status.

But purity extended beyond mere virginity. The truly pure woman was passionless, without sexual desire. Patmore's angel was "lacking any desire for sexual intercourse." Victorian ideology held that respectable women simply did not experience sexual feelings. If a woman did experience such feelings, she was by definition not respectable—she was closer to a prostitute than to an angel.

This ideology served male interests perfectly. It divided women into two categories: the pure (suitable for marriage and motherhood) and the impure (available for male sexual exploitation). It made women responsible for controlling male sexuality—any "fall" was the woman's fault, her failure to maintain proper boundaries. And it denied married women the right to refuse their husbands' sexual demands, since respectable women had no sexual desires of their own to consult.

Submissiveness

The true woman submitted to male authority without question. She obeyed her father until marriage, then transferred her obedience to her husband. She did not argue, did not assert her own opinions, did not challenge male decisions. She was, in the words of one conduct manual, "to give up her will, in all things in which principles and conscience are not at hazard."

Submissiveness was presented not as oppression but as fulfillment of women's nature. Women were naturally suited to follow; men were naturally suited to lead. A woman who submitted was merely accepting her proper role in the natural order. A woman who resisted was fighting against nature itself—and such resistance could only lead to unhappiness.

Women's rights advocates were condemned as "semi-women, mental hermaphrodites" who were "disrupting the natural order of things." They were accused not merely of being wrong but of being unnatural, of having lost their essential femininity through their unfeminine demands for equality.

Domesticity

The home was woman's "proper sphere," and she was to remain within it. Her duties were household management, child-rearing, and the creation of a peaceful, moral, comfortable refuge for her husband. These were not trivial tasks—domestic ideology elevated them to sacred calling. The home was a "temple" of virtue, and the wife was its "priestess."

But elevation was also confinement. The woman who stepped outside her sphere—who sought education, employment, or political participation—was violating her nature and endangering her family. The domestic sphere was not merely where women belonged; it was the only place they could properly exist. Outside it, they were fish out of water, beings operating in an environment for which nature had not designed them.

This ideology of domesticity privatized women's entire existence. Their work was unpaid, their opinions private, their influence limited to the domestic circle. They could not vote, hold office, own property (in most jurisdictions), or participate in public life. They were citizens of a separate nation—the nation of the home—over which they had symbolic authority but from which they could never emigrate.

• • •

Evidence for the Prosecution: GOD

The cult of domesticity drew its ultimate authority from claims about nature and divine design. Women's domestic role was not a social arrangement that might be changed; it was a natural fact as immutable as the difference between male and female bodies. To challenge it was to challenge nature itself—and nature's God.

The Theology of Separate Spheres

Victorian religious thought provided elaborate justifications for women's domestic confinement. God had created men and women differently, with different capacities and different purposes. Man was designed for the public sphere: rational, competitive, suited for commerce, politics, and intellectual pursuits. Woman was designed for the private sphere: emotional, nurturing, suited for homemaking, child-rearing, and moral influence.

These differences were not merely physical but spiritual. Man's soul was rational; woman's soul was emotional. Man's virtue was active—doing, achieving, building. Woman's virtue was passive—being, nurturing, supporting. Each was incomplete without the other, but they complemented each other only in their proper roles. A woman who tried to develop masculine virtues destroyed her feminine nature without gaining masculine capacity. She became, in the words of numerous commentators, a "monstrosity."

Evangelical Christianity was particularly influential in propagating separate spheres ideology. Thomas Gisborne's "An Enquiry into the Duties of the Female Sex" (1797) and Henry Venn's "The Complete Duty of Man" (1763) were widely read texts that described proper behavior for men and women, arguing that a woman's primary duty was to care for those in her domestic circle and obey her husband. These religious teachings reached deep into society, shaping expectations and constraining choices.

The Science of Sexual Difference

The nineteenth century saw the emergence of scientific authority as a complement to—and eventually replacement for—religious authority.

And science, as constructed by male scientists, confirmed what religion had taught: women were naturally suited for domesticity and naturally unsuited for public life.

Phrenologists claimed that the shape of women's skulls indicated limited rational capacity. Biologists argued that women's reproductive functions consumed so much energy that intellectual development would endanger their ability to bear children. Physicians warned that education would cause women's wombs to atrophy and their minds to break down. Evolutionary theorists argued that sexual difference was the product of millions of years of natural selection, with men evolving for competition and women for nurturing.

None of this was good science. The phrenologists were wrong about brain function. The biologists were wrong about energy conservation. The physicians were wrong about the effects of education. The evolutionary theorists were projecting contemporary social arrangements onto the prehistoric past. But it all served to give the cult of domesticity the imprimatur of scientific authority, making it seem not like ideology but like fact.

The Sacralization of Motherhood

The cult of domesticity elevated motherhood to the highest calling a woman could achieve. Mothers were the "backbone of Western Christian society," responsible for instilling piety and morals in the next generation. The fate of civilization depended on mothers properly fulfilling their duties.

This elevation was also entrapment. Motherhood was not a choice but a destiny, not one role among many but the defining purpose of female existence. A woman who did not become a mother was unfulfilled, incomplete, a failure. A woman who became a mother but sought other roles was neglecting her sacred duty. A woman who prioritized anything over motherhood was unnatural.

GOD thus fulfilled his role in the Victorian Masculine Triad by providing theological justification for separate spheres (God designed men and women for different roles), scientific confirmation of natural sexual difference (nature made women unsuited for public life), and sacred elevation of motherhood that was also imprisonment (motherhood as destiny, not choice).

• • •

Evidence for the Prosecution: THE DEVIL

Ideology would have been merely an annoyance if it had not been backed by law, medicine, and social coercion. The cult of domesticity was enforced through legal disabilities that stripped women of rights, medical practices that pathologized deviation, and social pressures that destroyed the reputations and livelihoods of women who refused to conform.

The Legal Framework: Coverture Continues

In England and its legal descendants, including the United States, the doctrine of coverture remained in force throughout most of the nineteenth century. Upon marriage, a woman's legal existence was "suspended" or "incorporated and consolidated into that of the husband." As William Blackstone had explained in his influential *Commentaries on the Laws of England*:

> *"By marriage, the husband and wife are one person in*
> *law: that is, the very being or legal existence of the*
> *woman is suspended during the marriage, or at least is*

incorporated and consolidated into that of the husband:
under whose wing, protection, and cover, she performs
every thing."

The practical consequences were devastating. A married woman could not own property in her own name. Any property she brought into the marriage became her husband's. Any money she earned belonged to her husband. She could not enter into contracts, could not sue or be sued, could not make a will without her husband's consent. Even her body was not her own—marital rape was not recognized as a crime, since a wife was presumed to have given perpetual consent to sexual relations upon marriage.

The famous suffragist Millicent Fawcett experienced the absurdity of coverture firsthand when her purse was snatched by a thief in London. In court, she was shocked to hear the youth charged with stealing property belonging to "Henry Fawcett"—her husband. Her purse, her money, were legally his.

Reform came slowly and incompletely. The Married Women's Property Act of 1870 in England allowed wives to keep their own earnings and some inherited property. The more comprehensive Act of 1882 finally allowed married women to own, buy, and sell property in their own names and restored their separate legal identity. But even these reforms left intact the fundamental structure of male authority within marriage, and they came only after decades of feminist organizing against fierce resistance.

The Medical Framework: Hysteria and the Rest Cure

If law constrained women's external freedoms, medicine constrained their internal lives—their minds, their bodies, their very sense of self.

The nineteenth century saw the development of elaborate medical theories about women's nature, women's illnesses, and women's treatment that served to pathologize any deviation from domestic norms.

The diagnosis of "hysteria"—from the Greek word for uterus—captured the ideology perfectly. Hysteria was a disease to which women were uniquely susceptible because of their female biology. Its symptoms were protean: depression, anxiety, irritability, insomnia, nervousness, any emotional disturbance that made a woman difficult or troublesome. What these symptoms had in common was that they represented women failing to be properly feminine—failing to be cheerful, compliant, content with their domestic role.

The treatments for hysteria were designed to enforce compliance. The most famous was the "rest cure" developed by American neurologist Silas Weir Mitchell in the 1870s. The rest cure required complete bed rest, isolation from family and friends, prohibition of any intellectual activity (including reading and writing), a diet of fatty foods and milk, and massage. Women were to lie passively, consume, and wait for their doctors to pronounce them cured.

Mitchell explicitly connected his cure to domestic ideology. He believed that depression in women was caused by too much mental activity and not enough attention to domestic affairs. The cure was to strip away everything that distinguished a woman as an individual—her thoughts, her creativity, her social connections—and reduce her to a passive body to be fed and manipulated by (male) medical authority.

Charlotte Perkins Gilman, the feminist writer, experienced the rest cure firsthand and nearly lost her mind. Her semi-autobiographical story "The Yellow Wallpaper" (1892) depicts a woman driven to insanity by the very treatment that was supposed to cure her. The narrator is forbidden to write, forbidden to think, confined to a room with disturbing yellow wallpaper that becomes the focus of her deteriorating mental state. By the end of the story, she has descended into madness—the "cure" has produced the very illness it claimed to treat.

Gilman's story was not merely fiction. Mitchell had instructed her to "live as domestic a life as possible" and "never touch pen, brush or pencil as long as you live." She obeyed for three months and, in her words, came "perilously close to losing my mind." She recovered only by ignoring Mitchell's advice and returning to her intellectual work. Her purpose in writing "The Yellow Wallpaper," she later explained, was "not intended to drive people crazy, but to save people from being driven crazy" by treatments that enforced the cult of domesticity through medical authority.

The Social Framework: Reputation and Ruin

Law and medicine were buttressed by social enforcement. The cult of domesticity created a system of surveillance in which women policed themselves and each other, enforcing conformity through the power of reputation.

A woman's reputation was her most valuable asset and her most vulnerable point. A hint of sexual impropriety could ruin her—not merely socially but economically, since marriage was the primary means of economic security for middle-class women. A reputation for unwomanly behavior—for being "strong-minded," "mannish," or "unfeminine"—could make a woman unmarriageable, condemning her to spinsterhood and economic marginalization.

This system made women complicit in their own subordination. Mothers taught daughters the rules of feminine behavior. Wives enforced domestic ideology on other wives. Women who violated the norms were ostracized by other women as much as by men. The cult of domesticity created a closed system in which any attempt to escape was punished by those still inside.

THE DEVIL thus fulfilled his role in the Victorian Masculine Triad through legal disabilities (coverture stripping married women of property, contracts, and legal identity), medical pathologization (hysteria diagnosis and rest cure punishing deviation from domestic norms), and social enforcement (reputation system making women police themselves and each other).

• • •

Evidence for the Prosecution: MAN

The cult of domesticity served men's interests directly and comprehensively. It provided them with unpaid domestic labor, sexual access, economic control, and psychological validation. The men who propagated this ideology were not disinterested observers describing natural facts; they were interested parties justifying arrangements that benefited them.

The Male Authors of Domestic Ideology

The cult of domesticity was created and propagated primarily by men. Coventry Patmore wrote "The Angel in the House." John Ruskin wrote "Of Queens' Gardens" (1865), celebrating women's domestic influence while confining them to it. Male ministers preached separate spheres from pulpits. Male scientists produced studies proving women's natural limitations. Male physicians diagnosed hysteria and prescribed the rest cure. Male legislators maintained coverture and resisted women's property rights.

These men were not neutral experts applying their professional knowledge. They had personal stakes in maintaining female subordination. Patmore's angel was his own wife, whom he wanted to remain devoted to him. Ruskin's idealization of domestic womanhood coexisted with his notorious inability to consummate his own marriage and his later obsession with young girls. Mitchell's rest cure gave him (and other male physicians) enormous power over female patients—power that he explicitly connected to restoring proper gender relations.

The Economic Benefits to Men

The cult of domesticity provided men with free domestic labor. A wife managed the household, raised the children, cooked the meals, cleaned the house, nursed the sick, and performed countless other tasks—all without wages. This labor had enormous economic value, but because it occurred within the "private sphere," it was not recognized as work and was not compensated.

Meanwhile, men's labor in the "public sphere" was waged. Men earned money; women did not. Men controlled the family's economic resources; women had no independent economic existence. Even when women did earn money (as working-class women always had to do), the cult of domesticity defined their work as supplementary, temporary, and unfortunate—not real work like men's work.

This economic arrangement made women dependent on men. A woman needed a husband (or father) for economic survival. She had little bargaining power within the relationship because she had no economic alternatives. If her husband was abusive, improvident, or simply disagreeable, she had limited options for escape. The cult of domesticity was not just ideology; it was a system of economic coercion.

The Sexual Benefits to Men

The purity ideology at the heart of domestic womanhood served men's sexual interests in multiple ways. It divided women into respectable women (suitable for marriage) and fallen women (available for exploitation). It placed responsibility for sexual morality on women, freeing men from accountability for their own desires. It denied respectable women any sexual agency, making them passive recipients of male desire rather than active participants with their own wishes.

Within marriage, the passionless ideal served husbands' interests. A wife who had no sexual desires of her own was obligated to serve her husband's desires. She could not refuse him because she had no competing desires to assert. She could not demand her own satisfaction because she was not supposed to have desires that required satisfaction. The marital bed was for the husband's pleasure; the wife's role was to submit.

The Psychological Benefits to Men

The cult of domesticity provided men with psychological validation. The angel in the house existed to make her husband feel important, to admire him, to comfort him, to affirm his masculine identity. She was, in effect, a mirror that reflected back a flattering image of male superiority.

Men returning from the competitive, amoral world of commerce and industry came home to a haven where they were lords, where their authority was unquestioned, where they could enjoy the deference and admiration that the outside world did not provide. The domestic sphere was not merely women's prison; it was men's palace, a space where male ego could flourish unchallenged.

MAN thus fulfilled his role in the Victorian Masculine Triad by creating and propagating domestic ideology (male writers, ministers, scientists, and physicians), extracting economic benefits (unpaid domestic labor and economic control), securing sexual advantages (passionless ideal serving male desires), and enjoying psychological gratification (domestic sphere as space of male ego validation).

• • •

The Class Dimensions of Domesticity

The cult of domesticity was primarily a middle-class and upper-class phenomenon. Working-class women could not afford to be angels in the house; they had to work for wages, whether in factories, as domestic servants, or in other occupations. The ideology of true womanhood was, in practice, an ideology of privileged womanhood.

But this did not exempt working-class women from its effects. They were measured against a standard they could not meet and found wanting. Their work was evidence not of necessity but of moral failure —their own or their husbands'. They were available for exploitation precisely because they had failed to achieve the protective status of domestic womanhood.

Similarly, the cult of domesticity was largely a white phenomenon. Black women, immigrant women, and other marginalized groups were excluded from the definition of "true womanhood" even as they were held to its standards. They were deemed naturally less pure, less pious, less suited for the domestic pedestal. Their exclusion justified their exploitation while reinforcing the racial hierarchy that intersected with gender subordination.

The class and racial dimensions of domesticity reveal its true nature. It was not a universal description of female nature but an ideology that served particular interests—the interests of privileged men in maintaining their privilege, and the interests of privileged women in distinguishing themselves from the unprivileged masses. The cult of domesticity was not merely sexist; it was a component of a larger system of social hierarchy that used gender, class, and race to maintain power.

• • •

Resistance and Its Costs

Women resisted the cult of domesticity throughout the nineteenth century. They organized for property rights, education, and suffrage. They wrote novels and essays challenging domestic ideology. They entered professions despite enormous obstacles. They created alternative communities and ways of living.

But resistance came at enormous cost. Women who challenged domestic norms were attacked as unwomanly, unnatural, and dangerous. They were denied employment, excluded from education, and ostracized from respectable society. They faced ridicule, harassment, and sometimes violence.

Frances Wright, one of the early advocates for women's rights, was denounced as a "female monster" and a "bold blasphemer." Harriet Martineau was called unfeminine for her intellectual work. The women of the Seneca Falls Convention in 1848 were mocked and condemned for their declaration of women's rights. The suffragists who followed were portrayed as ugly, mannish, and sexually deviant—as if the desire for political equality was evidence of biological abnormality.

The costs of resistance ensured that most women complied, or at least appeared to comply. They performed the role of angel in the house even if they chafed against its constraints. They taught their daughters the rules even if they privately questioned them. They enforced the norms on others even as they suffered under those norms themselves. The cult of domesticity was so thoroughly enforced that it seemed not like coercion but like nature—the way things were and had to be.

• • •

The Legacy of Domesticity

The cult of domesticity did not end with the Victorian era. Its influence extended well into the twentieth century and continues to shape expectations and arrangements today.

The "separate spheres" ideology persisted long after its religious and scientific justifications had been discredited. Women gained the vote, entered higher education, and moved into the workforce—yet the assumption that home was their "natural" sphere remained powerful. The "cult of domesticity" was renamed the "feminine mystique" by Betty Friedan in 1963, but its essential features persisted: the idealization of homemaking and motherhood, the devaluation of women's public achievements, the assumption that women's fulfillment came through serving others rather than developing themselves.

Even today, women perform far more unpaid domestic labor than men. Women are still expected to be the primary caregivers for children and elderly relatives. Women who prioritize career over family are still judged more harshly than men who do the same. The "angel in the house" has been updated for the modern era—she now might also have a career—but the expectation that women should put others' needs before their own remains deeply embedded in culture and psychology.

The Masculine Triad adapted the cult of domesticity to each new era, adjusting its justifications while maintaining its essential structure. When religious authority weakened, scientific authority took its place. When legal disabilities were removed, social and economic pressures remained. When explicit ideology was challenged, implicit assumptions persisted. The angel in the house changed her wardrobe, but she remained trapped in the house.

Understanding the cult of domesticity is essential to understanding how gender subordination operates. It was not a matter of brute force (though force was used when necessary). It was a matter of ideology that seemed like nature, of constraints that felt like choices, of oppression that presented itself as elevation. The angel's wings were clipped, but she was told she was flying.

CHAPTER TWELVE

Property and Personhood

In the 1860s, the suffragist Millicent Fawcett was walking through London when a young thief snatched her purse. The boy was caught and brought before the magistrate. Fawcett, expecting to testify about her stolen property, was startled to hear the charge read aloud: the boy had stolen a purse containing money "the property of Henry Fawcett"—her husband.

It was her purse. It was her money. But under the law, neither belonged to her. Upon marriage, everything Millicent Fawcett owned had become her husband's property. Her earnings were his. Her possessions were his. Even the clothes on her back legally belonged to him. She was, in the eyes of the law, not a person at all—merely an extension of her husband.

This was the doctrine of coverture: the legal principle that, upon marriage, a woman's legal existence was "suspended" or "merged" into that of her husband. As William Blackstone, the great eighteenth-century commentator on English law, explained: "The husband and wife are one person in law: that is, the very being or legal existence of the woman is suspended during the marriage, or at least is incorporated and consolidated into that of the husband."

Coverture was not a metaphor. It was a legal reality that shaped every aspect of a married woman's existence. She could not own property. She could not sign contracts. She could not sue or be sued. She could not keep her own earnings. She could not make a will. She could not even be the legal guardian of her own children. In the most fundamental sense, she did not exist as a person under the law.

This chapter examines the connection between property and personhood—how the denial of property rights functioned as a denial of legal existence, and how the long struggle for married women's property rights was simultaneously a struggle for recognition as human beings with independent existence. It is a story of law as instrument of oppression, of deliberate legal architecture designed to maintain male power, and of the women who fought to dismantle it.

• • •

The Architecture of Legal Death

Coverture was not merely a disadvantage or a disability. It was, in legal terms, a form of death. A married woman was sometimes described as "civilly dead"—alive in body but nonexistent in law. This legal death had comprehensive consequences.

Property and Earnings

When a woman married, everything she owned became her husband's property. If she had inherited money from her parents, it was now his. If she had owned a house, it was now his. If she had jewelry, clothing, books—all his. Any property she might acquire during marriage also belonged to him. Her wages, if she worked, were his wages. Her inheritance, if she received one, was his inheritance.

The husband could do whatever he wished with this property. He could spend it, sell it, give it away, gamble it, waste it—and his wife had no legal recourse. He could leave it in his will to someone other than her. He could use it to support his mistress. He could squander her entire inheritance on failed business ventures and she could do nothing to stop him.

A woman might enter marriage with a substantial fortune and leave it penniless, entirely through her husband's mismanagement, and have no legal claim to anything. The fortune that her parents had worked to accumulate, that might have been intended to provide for her throughout her life, could be dissipated in a matter of years by a husband over whom she had no control.

Contracts and Legal Actions

Because a married woman had no legal existence, she could not enter into contracts. She could not buy or sell property. She could not run a business in her own name. She could not borrow money or extend credit. She could not sue anyone for anything—if someone harmed her, her husband had to bring the suit. She could not be sued either, which meant that no one would extend her credit because there was no legal way to collect a debt from her.

This incapacity extended even to the most basic transactions. A married woman could not, strictly speaking, legally purchase groceries. Every transaction she made was legally made by her husband through her. She was not a party to contracts but merely an agent acting on behalf of her husband, the only actual legal person in the marriage.

Children

Perhaps the cruelest aspect of coverture was its treatment of children. Under common law, the father was the sole legal guardian of any children born within the marriage. The mother had no legal rights to her own children whatsoever.

This meant that a father could take the children away from their mother at any time, for any reason or no reason at all. He could send them to live with relatives. He could send them to boarding schools. He could even, as some fathers did, send them to live with his mistress. The mother could not stop him. She could not sue for custody. She could not even legally visit her children without her husband's permission.

If the marriage ended through separation or the husband's death, the situation could become even worse. A father could appoint anyone he chose to be the guardian of his children after his death—and that person did not have to be the mother. He could specify in his will that the children should never see their mother again, and the courts would enforce this provision.

The case that galvanized reform illustrates the human cost of these rules. Caroline Norton, a well-known writer and society figure in 1830s England, separated from her abusive husband George Norton. He immediately took their three sons and refused to let her see them. When she tried to visit, the children were moved. When she sent letters, they were returned unopened. She had no legal remedy because she had no legal rights to her own children.

For years, Caroline Norton campaigned for reform, publishing pamphlets that documented the injustice of a system that gave a mother "no rights at all, whatever the behaviour of the husband." Her efforts eventually led to the Custody of Infants Act 1839, which allowed mothers to petition for custody of children under seven years old—if the mother had not been found guilty of adultery. It was a tiny crack in the wall of paternal absolute authority, won through enormous effort and applying only in limited circumstances.

The Body

Coverture extended even to a woman's physical person. A husband had legal rights over his wife's body that she could not refuse. Marital rape was not recognized as a crime—indeed, the concept was considered logically impossible, since a wife was deemed to have given irrevocable consent to sexual relations upon marriage. A husband could legally force his wife to have sex against her will, and no court would intervene.

Husbands also retained the legal right to "chastise" their wives—to use physical force to correct them—although this right was increasingly questioned as the nineteenth century progressed. The old rule of thumb supposedly allowing a husband to beat his wife with a stick no thicker than his thumb was never clearly established in English law, but the general principle that husbands could use "moderate correction" persisted.

A wife could not leave her husband without his permission. If she did, he could legally compel her return. Courts would issue writs requiring a wife to return to her husband's home and submit to his authority. A woman fleeing an abusive husband had no legal right to leave and could be forced back into his household.

• • •

Evidence for the Prosecution: GOD

Coverture was justified as natural, necessary, and divinely ordained. The legal doctrine was supported by an elaborate ideology that presented male authority over women as part of the natural order, established by God and confirmed by nature.

The Unity of Person

The theological foundation of coverture rested on the idea that marriage made husband and wife "one flesh." This biblical concept was translated into legal terms: if husband and wife were one person, then that one person must have one legal identity—and that identity was the husband's.

Blackstone explained the principle: "Upon this principle, of an union of person in husband and wife, depend almost all the legal rights, duties, and disabilities, that either of them acquire by the marriage." The unity of person was not just a legal fiction; it was presented as a spiritual reality with legal consequences.

This theological justification made coverture seem not like oppression but like the natural order of things. The wife's subordination was not arbitrary male power; it was the fulfillment of divine design. To challenge coverture was to challenge God's plan for marriage and the family.

Protection and Dependence

Coverture was also justified as protection. A woman was "under the wing, protection, and cover" of her husband, "her baron, or lord." She was dependent on him, and in return for her dependence, he protected her. The disability was presented as a benefit.

Blackstone argued that "even the disabilities, which the wife lies under, are for the most part intended for her protection and benefit. So great a favorite is the female sex of the laws of England." The woman who could not own property, could not sue, could not control her own earnings—she was supposedly a "favorite" of the law because the law protected her by placing her under male authority.

This ideological framework made it difficult to argue for reform. If coverture was protection, then removing it was exposing women to danger. If coverture reflected natural dependence, then changing it was fighting against nature. The ideology of protection masked the reality of subordination.

Natural Difference

By the nineteenth century, the theological justifications for coverture were supplemented with arguments from nature and science. Men and women were naturally different, the argument went. Men were suited for the public sphere—for business, law, politics. Women were suited for the private sphere—for home, children, domestic management. Coverture merely recognized these natural differences and organized society accordingly.

This naturalizing of coverture made it seem eternal and unchangeable. Legal rules could be modified; natural facts could not. If women's subordination was natural, then any attempt to change it was doomed to fail—or worse, would create unnatural women and disordered families.

GOD thus fulfilled his role in the coverture system by providing theological justification (unity of person as divine design), ideological cover (subordination presented as protection), and naturalization (legal rules presented as natural facts).

• • •

Evidence for the Prosecution: THE DEVIL

Coverture was not merely an ideology; it was a comprehensive legal system that shaped every aspect of a married woman's life. The law actively constructed women's subordination, created the conditions of their dependence, and punished any attempt to escape.

The Legal Architecture

English common law developed coverture over centuries, creating an intricate system of rules that left married women with virtually no independent legal existence. This was not accident or oversight; it was deliberate legal construction.

The rules were comprehensive: a married woman's real property (land) came under her husband's control, though he could not sell it without her consent (in theory to protect her dower rights after his death). Her personal property (everything else) became absolutely his, to dispose of as he wished. Her earnings were his. Her contracts were void. Her legal actions required his participation. Her children were his.

The system was internally consistent and mutually reinforcing. Because a woman could not own property, she could not support herself independently. Because she could not support herself, she was dependent on her husband. Because she was dependent on her husband, she had no bargaining power in the relationship. Because she had no bargaining power, she could not negotiate better terms. The legal rules created the conditions of dependence and then pointed to that dependence as justification for the rules.

Equity's Partial Remedy

The harshness of common law coverture was somewhat moderated by courts of equity, which developed alternative legal devices. Wealthy families could create "separate estates" through trusts, placing property in the hands of trustees who would manage it for the wife's benefit rather than allowing it to be absorbed by the husband.

But these equity remedies were available only to the wealthy. Creating a trust required lawyers, trustees, and property substantial enough to be worth the legal expense. Working-class women and women without family wealth had no access to these protections. The ability to evade coverture was itself a class privilege.

Moreover, even equity did not fully restore women's legal personality. A woman with a separate estate still could not vote, could not hold office, could not serve on juries. The separate estate protected her property; it did not make her a full legal person.

Reform's Slow Progress

Reform came slowly and grudgingly. Each small change required years of campaigning and was met with fierce resistance from those who defended coverture as natural and necessary.

The Custody of Infants Act of 1839 allowed mothers who had not committed adultery to petition for custody of children under seven. The Matrimonial Causes Act of 1857 created a new divorce court and gave some property rights to divorced and separated women. The Married Women's Property Act of 1870 allowed women to keep their own earnings and some inherited property. The more comprehensive Married Women's Property Act of 1882 finally gave married women the same property rights as unmarried women.

Each of these reforms was incomplete. The 1839 act applied only to children under seven; only to mothers who had not committed adultery (while adulterous fathers retained full rights); and did not apply in Scotland, allowing Caroline Norton's husband to evade it by moving the children there. The 1870 act was so limited that reformers immediately began campaigning for its replacement. The 1882 act restored property rights but did not address voting rights, custody rights, or countless other disabilities.

The legal death of married women was ended not by a single stroke but by a thousand cuts, each one requiring enormous effort and each one leaving some portion of the old system intact.

THE DEVIL thus fulfilled his role in the coverture system by creating and maintaining comprehensive legal architecture (the system of rules that constituted married women's legal death), providing limited remedies that reinforced class privilege (equity's separate estates available only to the wealthy), and resisting reform at every stage (each small change requiring years of campaigning against fierce opposition).

• • •

Evidence for the Prosecution: MAN

Coverture served men's interests comprehensively. It gave husbands control over their wives' property, earnings, bodies, and children. It made wives economically dependent on their husbands. It gave husbands power within the marriage that they could exercise without accountability.

Economic Benefits

The most obvious benefit of coverture to men was economic. When a man married, he gained control of everything his wife owned and everything she might acquire. If he married a wealthy woman, he became wealthy. If his wife worked, her earnings were his. If she inherited property, it was his property.

This created incentives for men to marry for money. The fortune-hunter—the man who married a wealthy woman to gain access to her property—was a stock figure in nineteenth-century literature precisely because coverture made such hunting profitable. A man with no money of his own could become rich through marriage, while the woman who had been wealthy before marriage might find herself with nothing after her husband squandered her inheritance.

Coverture also protected men from the economic consequences of their own failures. A husband could use his wife's money to pay his debts. He could use her property as collateral for loans. He could maintain his social position and his business ventures using resources that she had brought to the marriage. His financial risks were cushioned by her property; her property was exposed to his risks.

Power Within Marriage

Coverture gave husbands enormous power over their wives—power that could be used benevolently or abusively, but that was always there as background fact of the marriage.

A husband who controlled all the family's property controlled his wife's access to the necessities of life. He could give her an allowance or not. He could permit her to purchase things or not. He could be generous or stingy, and she had no recourse either way. Even if she earned money through her own labor, that money was his to dispose of as he wished.

This economic control translated into control over every aspect of married life. A wife who depended on her husband for every penny was in a weak negotiating position on every question. She could not threaten to leave because she had no independent resources. She could not refuse unreasonable demands because refusal might result in being cut off from access to money. The economic structure of coverture created the conditions for domination even when husbands did not consciously intend to dominate.

The Absence of Accountability

Perhaps most significantly, coverture meant that husbands exercised their power without accountability. There was no one to whom they had to answer for how they treated their wives, how they spent the family's money, how they raised the children.

A wife could not sue her husband—suing would require that she have legal existence separate from him, which coverture denied. A wife could not testify against her husband in most circumstances. A wife could not go to court to complain about his management of her property because it was not legally her property anymore.

This absence of accountability meant that the law provided no check on a husband's exercise of power. Good husbands might voluntarily treat their wives well, might consult them about decisions, might manage property wisely. Bad husbands could do whatever they liked. The law provided no mechanism for distinguishing between them or for protecting wives from abuse of power.

MAN thus fulfilled his role in the coverture system by extracting economic benefits (control of wives' property and earnings), exercising power within marriage (economic dependence creating conditions for domination), and enjoying freedom from accountability (no legal mechanisms for checking husbands' exercise of power).

• • •

The Fight for Legal Personhood

Women did not accept their legal death quietly. From the earliest days of coverture, women and their allies challenged the system—

sometimes through legal maneuvering, sometimes through political campaigning, sometimes through the sheer force of publicizing injustice.

Individual Resistance

Many women found ways to work around coverture's restrictions. They ran businesses in their husbands' names, or under the legal fiction of being a "feme sole trader" (a married woman permitted to conduct business as if she were single). They managed property through informal arrangements that courts did not recognize but communities respected. They negotiated with husbands for allowances and some degree of autonomy.

These individual strategies were not political resistance, but they demonstrate that women did not simply accept coverture as natural or inevitable. They worked within and around the system, carving out spaces for agency even within a legal framework designed to deny them agency.

The Reform Campaigns

Organized campaigns for married women's rights emerged in the early nineteenth century and accelerated after 1848. In England, Caroline Norton's public campaign for child custody rights in the 1830s was one of the first sustained efforts to change the law. Her pamphlets documenting the injustices she had suffered—and that other women suffered—helped build public sympathy for reform.

In the United States, the Seneca Falls Convention of 1848 placed property rights at the center of the women's rights agenda. The Declaration of Sentiments, modeled on the Declaration of Independence, catalogued women's grievances, with property rights prominent among them:

"He has made her, if married, in the eye of the law, civilly dead. He has taken from her all right in property, even to the wages she earns."

The Declaration of Sentiments articulated what women had always known but what had rarely been stated so clearly: that coverture was not protection but oppression, not natural but artificial, not beneficial but harmful. It reframed the issue from one of male protection of dependent women to one of male domination of equal human beings.

The Legal Changes

The legal changes came slowly, over decades, and varied by jurisdiction. In the United States, Mississippi was the first state to pass a Married Women's Property Act, in 1839—motivated partly by the desire of slaveholding families to protect their property from creditors by placing it in their wives' names. New York passed its Married Women's Property Act in 1848, just months before the Seneca Falls Convention. Other states followed over the next several decades.

In England, the Married Women's Property Act of 1870 was a crucial first step, allowing women to keep their own earnings and certain inherited property. The 1882 act was more comprehensive, giving married women the same property rights as unmarried women. But even after 1882, vestiges of coverture remained—in voting rights (women could not vote in parliamentary elections until 1918), in jury service (women were not regularly allowed on juries until the 1960s), in marital rape (not recognized as a crime until 1991).

The ghost of coverture has never been fully exorcised. Even today, women encounter its remnants in real estate transactions, in tax matters, in various legal and bureaucratic contexts where the assumption of male headship persists.

•••

Property, Personhood, and Freedom

The connection between property and personhood was not incidental to coverture—it was its essence. To deny someone the right to own property is to deny them the material basis for independent existence. A person who cannot own anything is utterly dependent on those who can own things. They cannot leave bad situations because they have nowhere to go and nothing to take with them. They cannot make independent choices because they have no independent resources to back those choices up.

The women's rights advocates of the nineteenth century understood this connection clearly. Elizabeth Cady Stanton argued that "man is a social being who looks to his fellow man for support. Woman is a social being who looks to man for protection." The reformers sought to change this by giving women the economic independence that would allow them to be social beings in their own right, not dependent on male protection.

This is why property rights were so central to the early women's movement. Suffrage was important—the right to vote, to participate in political decisions—but without property rights, the vote itself would be meaningless. A woman who could not own property, could not keep her own earnings, could not enter contracts, was not really a citizen in any meaningful sense. She was a dependent, legally equivalent to a child or an incompetent.

The fight for property rights was thus a fight for personhood, for recognition as a human being with independent existence and worth. It was not merely about money or possessions; it was about the fundamental question of whether women were people or property, whether they had selves or were merely extensions of their husbands.

• • •

The Masculine Triad and Legal Death

Coverture demonstrates the Masculine Triad at its most systematic. It was a comprehensive legal system that created and enforced female subordination, backed by an ideology that made subordination seem natural and necessary.

God provided the ideological foundation: the theological concept of marital unity, the naturalization of male authority, the presentation of subordination as protection. These ideas made coverture seem not like human invention but like divine and natural law, beyond legitimate challenge.

The Devil provided the legal machinery: the detailed rules that stripped married women of property, contracts, legal actions, and custody of children; the courts that enforced these rules; the reluctance of legal institutions to reform a system that served their interests. This machinery was not neutral; it was constructed by men to serve male interests.

Man provided the beneficiaries: husbands who gained control of their wives' property and labor, who exercised power without accountability, who could treat their wives well or badly according to their own characters without legal constraint. The men who operated within this system—even the good ones, even the loving husbands who treated their wives kindly—benefited from a structure designed to maintain their dominance.

The fight against coverture was a fight against all three arms of the Triad. Reformers had to challenge the ideology that justified coverture as natural and beneficial. They had to change the legal rules that created married women's disabilities. And they had to overcome the resistance of men who benefited from the existing system.

This fight is ongoing. The legal death of married women was ended —mostly—by the reforms of the nineteenth and twentieth centuries. But the connection between property, personhood, and freedom remains relevant. Economic dependence still constrains women's choices. Legal and financial systems still sometimes treat women as appendages of their husbands. The assumption that men are the default human beings still pervades many institutions.

Understanding coverture helps us understand how law can create subordination, how ideology can make subordination seem natural, and how comprehensive systems of oppression can be dismantled only through sustained effort over generations. The married woman of the nineteenth century who could not own her purse is connected to the woman of the twenty-first century who still earns less, owns less, and has less power than her male counterparts. The fight for property and personhood continues.

CHAPTER THIRTEEN

The Long Road to Suffrage

On August 26, 1920, the Nineteenth Amendment to the United States Constitution was ratified, declaring that "the right of citizens of the United States to vote shall not be denied or abridged by the United States or by any State on account of sex." Alice Paul, the militant suffragist who had organized pickets, been imprisoned, gone on hunger strikes, and been force-fed through tubes, stood on a balcony and unfurled a banner with a star for each state that had ratified the amendment.

It had taken seventy-two years. From the Seneca Falls Convention in 1848 to ratification in 1920, the struggle for women's suffrage had consumed three generations of activists. Women who began the fight died before seeing victory. Daughters took up the work their mothers had started. Granddaughters finally saw the amendment ratified.

Seventy-two years. For perspective: that is longer than the entire existence of the Soviet Union from revolution to collapse. It is longer than the period from the Wright Brothers' first flight to the Moon landing. It is longer than most human lifetimes. The simple demand that women be allowed to vote—a right that had been extended to propertyless men, to former slaves, to immigrants who had just arrived in America—required three-quarters of a century of organizing, petitioning, marching, lobbying, and suffering before it was granted to half the population.

And even then, the victory was incomplete. For Black women in the South, the Nineteenth Amendment was largely meaningless. Poll taxes, literacy tests, grandfather clauses, and terrorist violence kept them from the polls for another forty-five years, until the Voting Rights Act of 1965. The suffrage movement's victory was a victory primarily for white women—and even that required seventy-two years of struggle against the Masculine Triad.

This chapter examines that struggle: the arguments against women's suffrage, the tactics used to delay and deny, and the ultimate victory that was both triumph and betrayal. It is a story of how the Masculine Triad operates when challenged directly, how it adapts and resists, and how even its defeats can be partial and conditional.

• • •

The Opposition

Women's suffrage was opposed not by a handful of reactionaries but by the mainstream of American and British society. Until 1916, more American women belonged to anti-suffrage organizations than to suffrage organizations. The opposition included men and women, conservatives and some progressives, religious leaders and secular intellectuals, the wealthy and the working class. It was, for most of the seventy-two years, the dominant position.

The Argument from Nature

The most fundamental argument against women's suffrage was that it violated the natural order. Men and women were created different, with different capacities and different spheres. Politics belonged to the male sphere; domesticity belonged to the female sphere. To give women the vote was to violate the natural division of labor between the sexes.

This argument was presented as obvious common sense. Of course women should not vote—they were women. Their nature suited them for the home, for nurturing children, for creating domestic peace. Politics was conflict, competition, corruption—the opposite of everything women were supposed to be and do. To drag women into the political arena was to drag them away from their natural calling and corrupt their essential nature.

The naturalization of gender difference made suffrage opposition seem not like prejudice but like wisdom. The anti-suffragists were not against women; they were for women—for protecting women from the degradation of political participation, for preserving their special role in society, for keeping them in the sphere where they belonged and could flourish.

The Argument from Protection

Related to the argument from nature was the argument from protection. Women did not need the vote because they were already protected by men. A woman's interests were represented by her husband, her father, her brothers. To give women a separate vote was to imply that their interests might conflict with those of the men who protected them—a dangerous and destabilizing idea.

This argument was particularly ironic given that the legal system—as we have seen with coverture—systematically denied married women independent legal existence. The same system that erased women's legal personhood now claimed to represent their interests through the men who controlled them. Women did not need their own voice because men spoke for them; and men spoke for them because women had no independent voice.

The Argument from Domestic Feminism

Some women opposed suffrage from what might be called a "domestic feminist" position. They believed that women had achieved a certain power and autonomy within the home and that entry into politics would actually diminish that power. Better to rule the domestic sphere absolutely than to be a minority voice in the public sphere.

This argument had some basis in reality. The ideology of separate spheres had given women moral authority within the home—authority that might be threatened if they entered the morally compromised world of politics. Some women genuinely believed that their influence was greater as the power behind the throne than it would be as one voter among millions.

But this argument also reflected internalized subordination. The women who opposed suffrage had learned to value the limited power they possessed and to fear the loss of that power more than they desired real equality. They had been taught that women's power lay in influence rather than authority, and they had come to believe it.

The Argument from Chaos

Anti-suffragists warned that giving women the vote would lead to social chaos. If women could vote, what was next? Would they serve on juries? Would they hold office? Would they become lawyers and doctors and businesswomen? Would they abandon their domestic duties? Would families fall apart as women pursued political ambitions?

This slippery slope argument was, of course, correct—women would indeed go on to serve on juries, hold office, and enter professions. The anti-suffragists were right that suffrage was the entering wedge for broader changes in women's status. They were wrong to call those changes chaos. But their fears reveal what was really at stake: not just the vote, but the entire system of gender hierarchy that the vote's denial both symbolized and reinforced.

• • •

Evidence for the Prosecution: GOD

The opposition to women's suffrage drew heavily on ideological resources—religious, scientific, and philosophical—that presented women's exclusion from politics as natural, necessary, and divinely ordained.

Religious Opposition

Religious leaders were among the most vocal opponents of women's suffrage. They cited biblical passages about women's submission to male authority, about women's role in the home, about the danger of women speaking in public. The churches taught that God had established male headship in the family and that this extended to male headship in society.

In Britain, Queen Victoria herself—the most powerful woman in the world—was implacably opposed to women's suffrage. Her opposition made it politically difficult for any government to advance the cause. How could Parliament grant women the vote when the Queen herself thought it a "mad, wicked folly"? The monarch who ruled an empire believed that women should not participate in choosing their representatives.

In Ireland, both Catholic and Protestant churches opposed women's suffrage. Religious authorities wanted women's influence to remain domestic. The churches that preached women's submission to their husbands also preached women's exclusion from political participation.

Scientific Justifications

By the late nineteenth century, scientific arguments supplemented religious ones. Scientists claimed that women's brains were smaller than men's, that women's reproductive functions left insufficient energy for intellectual pursuits, that evolution had suited women for nurturing and men for competition.

These scientific arguments were no more valid than the scientific racism of the same era. But they provided secular justification for religious conclusions. Even those who did not accept biblical authority could accept "scientific" evidence that women were naturally unsuited for political participation.

Philosophical Arguments

Philosophers and political theorists contributed their own arguments against women's suffrage. Even John Stuart Mill, one of the few prominent male intellectuals to support women's suffrage, faced ridicule when he presented a suffrage petition to Parliament in 1867. The dominant view was that citizenship and voting were male prerogatives, connected to military service and economic productivity in ways that excluded women.

The philosophical arguments often rested on circular reasoning. Women were excluded from the activities that qualified one for citizenship—military service, economic independence, political participation—and their exclusion was then cited as evidence that they were unsuited for citizenship. The system created the conditions it then pointed to as justification.

GOD thus fulfilled his role in the suffrage opposition by providing religious justification (biblical arguments for male authority and women's domestic role), scientific cover (claims about women's natural incapacity for politics), and philosophical respectability (theories of citizenship that excluded women by definition).

• • •

Evidence for the Prosecution: THE DEVIL

Ideology would have been merely irritating if it had not been backed by the machinery of government. The suffragists faced not just arguments but institutional opposition: legislatures that refused to act, courts that ruled against them, police who arrested them, prisons that brutalized them.

Legislative Obstruction

The suffragists' primary tactic for decades was to petition legislatures for the right to vote. They collected millions of signatures. They testified before committees. They lobbied individual legislators. And for decades, legislatures simply refused to act.

In Britain, suffrage bills were introduced repeatedly in Parliament and defeated repeatedly—or simply not brought to a vote. Neither major political party would commit to women's suffrage because neither wanted to alienate voters who opposed it. The women had no votes to offer in exchange for politicians' support; the politicians had every incentive to ignore them.

In the United States, the suffragists pursued a state-by-state strategy as well as a federal amendment. Some western states granted women the vote—Wyoming Territory in 1869, Colorado in 1893—but most states refused. The federal amendment, first introduced in 1878, was defeated year after year in Congress.

The legislative obstruction was not passive. Legislators actively worked to prevent women's suffrage. They used procedural tricks to avoid votes. They amended bills to make them unacceptable. They delayed and postponed and tabled. The machinery of democracy was used to prevent democracy's expansion.

Police Repression

When suffragists moved from petitioning to direct action, they faced police repression. In Britain, the Women's Social and Political Union (WSPU), led by Emmeline Pankhurst and her daughters, adopted militant tactics: disrupting political meetings, smashing windows, damaging property, setting fires. The government responded with arrests, imprisonment, and brutality.

In the United States, Alice Paul and the National Woman's Party organized pickets outside the White House—the first political protests ever held there. When America entered World War I in 1917, the picketers were arrested for "obstructing traffic." They were sent to the Occoquan Workhouse in Virginia, where conditions were brutal.

The imprisoned suffragists demanded to be treated as political prisoners. When they were refused, they went on hunger strikes. The government's response was force-feeding—a brutal procedure in which tubes were forced down the prisoners' throats or into their nostrils and liquid food was poured in. Alice Paul was force-fed repeatedly. Doctors threatened to commit her to an insane asylum.

The "Night of Terror" on November 15, 1917, saw guards at Occoquan beat, choke, and brutalize imprisoned suffragists. Women were dragged, thrown against walls, chained to cell bars. The violence was authorized by prison officials and designed to break the women's resistance.

The Government's Dilemma

The government faced a dilemma. If it ignored the suffragists, their protests would continue. If it arrested them, it created martyrs. If it force-fed hunger strikers, it generated sympathy. If it released them, they resumed protesting.

In Britain, the government passed the "Cat and Mouse Act" in 1913, which allowed hunger-striking prisoners to be released when their health deteriorated and re-arrested when they recovered. This cynical legislation was designed to avoid the political cost of suffragists dying in prison while still punishing them for their protests.

Eventually, the government's brutality backfired. Reports of force-feeding and the Night of Terror generated public outrage. The spectacle of the American government torturing women for demanding the right to vote—while simultaneously fighting a war for democracy abroad—was too much cognitive dissonance to sustain. Public opinion shifted, and with it, political calculation.

THE DEVIL thus fulfilled his role in the suffrage opposition through legislative obstruction (years of refusing to vote on suffrage bills or defeating them when voted upon), police repression (arrests, imprisonment, and brutality against peaceful protesters), and strategic violence (force-feeding and physical abuse designed to break women's resistance while avoiding the political cost of their deaths).

• • •

Evidence for the Prosecution: MAN

The opposition to women's suffrage was overwhelmingly male. Men controlled the legislatures that refused to grant suffrage. Men ran the police forces that arrested suffragists. Men operated the prisons that brutalized them. And men had obvious interests in maintaining their monopoly on political power.

The Male Monopoly on Politics

Before women's suffrage, politics was an exclusively male domain. Men voted, men held office, men made laws, men enforced them. This monopoly gave men collective power over women—the power to determine women's legal rights, to define the conditions of marriage and divorce, to control women's property and earnings, to decide whether and when women could enter professions.

Women's suffrage threatened this monopoly. If women could vote, they could influence who held office. If they could influence who held office, they could affect what laws were passed. If they could affect what laws were passed, they could change the conditions of their own subordination. The stakes were not merely symbolic; they were material and concrete.

The Anti-Suffrage Men

Men organized against women's suffrage just as women did. They formed anti-suffrage leagues. They funded anti-suffrage publications. They gave anti-suffrage speeches. They used their institutional power— in churches, universities, businesses, and government—to oppose the extension of the franchise to women.

The men who opposed suffrage were not a marginal group. They included presidents (Woodrow Wilson opposed suffrage until 1918), prime ministers (William Gladstone opposed it throughout his long career), religious leaders, business leaders, and ordinary men who simply believed that politics was their domain and women should stay out of it.

The Benefits of Exclusion

Men benefited from women's exclusion from politics in multiple ways. Most directly, they did not have to compete with women for political power. But the benefits extended further. Laws that subordinated women—coverture, restrictions on employment and education, unequal divorce laws—could be maintained because women had no voice in changing them. The political system that excluded women also governed women, and the men who controlled that system had every reason to keep it that way.

MAN thus fulfilled his role in the suffrage opposition by maintaining political monopoly (exclusive male control of voting, office-holding, and law-making), organizing opposition (anti-suffrage leagues and publications), and benefiting from exclusion (using political power to maintain laws that subordinated women).

• • •

The Movement's Internal Divisions

The suffrage movement was not unified, and its internal divisions reveal uncomfortable truths about the limits of solidarity among women and about the ways that one form of oppression can be used to advance another.

The Fifteenth Amendment Split

In 1870, the Fifteenth Amendment to the Constitution was ratified, prohibiting the denial of voting rights based on "race, color, or previous condition of servitude." It did not mention sex. Black men—at least in theory—gained the right to vote. Women did not.

This created a bitter split in the women's movement. Frederick Douglass, the great abolitionist who had supported women's suffrage at Seneca Falls, argued that this was "the Negro's hour"—that Black men's voting rights should not be delayed for the sake of women's suffrage. Elizabeth Cady Stanton and Susan B. Anthony disagreed. They opposed the Fifteenth Amendment because it excluded women, and in their opposition, they deployed racist arguments that would taint the suffrage movement for decades.

Stanton complained about giving the vote to "Patrick and Sambo and Hans and Yung Tung, who do not know the difference between a monarchy and a republic, who cannot read the Declaration of Independence," while educated white women remained disenfranchised. The movement that had emerged from abolitionism was now using racist rhetoric to advance its cause.

Racism in the Movement

The racism was not incidental. Many white suffragists, especially in the South, explicitly argued for women's suffrage as a way to increase white political power. If white women could vote, they would outnumber Black voters. Women's suffrage could be a tool of white supremacy.

This racism had practical consequences for Black women in the movement. At the 1913 suffrage parade in Washington, D.C., organized by Alice Paul, Black women were asked to march at the back of the procession so as not to offend Southern white women. Ida B.

Wells, the great anti-lynching activist and suffragist, refused. She waited until the parade began and then joined her state's delegation, marching where she belonged rather than where racism demanded.

The National American Woman Suffrage Association (NAWSA) excluded Black women from its conventions. White suffragists chose not to integrate issues of race into their campaigns. They ignored the fact that Black women faced both racism and sexism, that their exclusion was doubly determined, that their need for the vote was even greater than white women's.

Black Women's Suffrage Work

Black women organized their own suffrage movement within and alongside the white-dominated organizations. Ida B. Wells founded the Alpha Suffrage Club of Chicago in 1913, the first Black women's suffrage club in Illinois. Mary Church Terrell, Frances Ellen Watkins Harper, Sojourner Truth, and countless others worked for suffrage while also fighting racism—sometimes fighting racism within the suffrage movement itself.

As Adella Hunt Logan of Tuskegee argued: "If white American women, with all their natural and acquired advantages, need the ballot, how much more do Black Americans, male and female, need the strong defense of a vote to help secure their right to life, liberty and the pursuit of happiness?"

Black women understood that the Nineteenth Amendment, if passed, would not actually give them the vote in the South. The same mechanisms that prevented Black men from voting—poll taxes, literacy tests, grandfather clauses, and outright violence—would prevent Black women from voting too. Their fight would have to continue long after 1920.

•••

Victory and Its Limits

The Nineteenth Amendment was ratified on August 26, 1920. Seventy-two years after Seneca Falls, American women had won the right to vote. But the victory was both less and more than it appeared.

Less Than It Appeared

For Black women in the South, the Nineteenth Amendment changed little. The same Jim Crow mechanisms that had disenfranchised Black men since the 1890s now applied to Black women. Poll taxes, literacy tests, understanding clauses, grandfather clauses, and white primaries kept Black citizens from voting regardless of the Constitution's guarantees.

And behind the legal mechanisms stood terrorist violence. The Ku Klux Klan and similar organizations used murder, assault, and intimidation to prevent Black political participation. A Black woman who tried to register to vote might lose her job, her home, or her life. The Nineteenth Amendment's promise of suffrage "not denied or abridged on account of sex" was hollow when it could be denied on account of race.

It would take another forty-five years—until the Voting Rights Act of 1965—for Black women to exercise the franchise in practice. The suffrage movement's victory was a victory for white women; Black women would have to continue fighting.

More Than It Appeared

At the same time, the Nineteenth Amendment was more than just the vote. It represented a fundamental shift in the conception of citizenship. Women were now voters, citizens in the full political sense. They could not be dismissed as mere dependents whose interests were represented by their husbands. They were political actors in their own right.

This shift had consequences beyond voting. Women who could vote could also run for office, serve on juries, participate in party politics. The Nineteenth Amendment did not create full equality, but it established the principle of equal political participation—a principle that would be invoked in later struggles for women's rights.

The suffragists had also demonstrated something important about resistance. They had shown that persistent, organized opposition could eventually overcome even deeply entrenched systems of exclusion. The tactics they developed—petitions, lobbying, demonstrations, civil disobedience, hunger strikes—would be adopted by later movements for civil rights and social change.

• • •

The Masculine Triad's Adaptation

The suffrage struggle illustrates how the Masculine Triad operates when directly challenged—and how it adapts when defeat becomes inevitable.

For seventy-two years, the Triad successfully resisted women's suffrage. GOD provided the ideological justification: women's natural role was domestic, their nature unsuited for politics, their place determined by divine and natural law. THE DEVIL provided the institutional resistance: legislatures that refused to act, police that arrested protesters, prisons that brutalized them. MAN benefited from the exclusion and organized to maintain it.

But when victory became inevitable, the Triad adapted. The Nineteenth Amendment was passed with the support of politicians who had long opposed it, including President Wilson, who announced his support only in 1918. The opposition did not convert to feminism; it calculated that resistance was no longer tenable and that cooperation might allow it to shape the terms of defeat.

And the Triad's adaptation continued after ratification. The same Southern states that had fought suffrage now used racist mechanisms to ensure that the amendment would benefit only white women. The political parties that had resisted women's suffrage now worked to channel women's political participation into acceptable forms. The victory was real, but it was also managed—contained within limits that preserved as much of the old order as possible.

This pattern—resistance followed by adaptation, defeat followed by containment—recurs throughout the history of women's rights. The Masculine Triad does not surrender; it retreats to more defensible positions. It does not accept equality; it grants concessions while maintaining hierarchy. Each victory is real, but each victory is also incomplete, leaving work for the next generation.

The suffragists who stood on that balcony in August 1920, watching Alice Paul unfurl her victory banner, had won something important. But they knew—or should have known—that the fight was not over. The right to vote was a beginning, not an end. The Masculine Triad had lost a battle, but it had not surrendered the war.

CHAPTER FOURTEEN

The Second Wave and Its Enemies

The prosecution now turns to the contemporary period. In Part IV, we will demonstrate that the Masculine Triad did not disappear with legal reforms—it adapted. As women gained formal rights, GOD, THE DEVIL, and MAN developed new strategies to maintain the substance of subordination even as its forms evolved. The evidence will show that every feminist advance has been met with organized resistance, and that the battle continues today.

In 1960, the typical American woman lived a life that would have been recognizable to her grandmother. She married young, bore children, and devoted herself to home and family. She could not get a credit card in her own name. If she worked outside the home, she was paid less than men for the same work—and that was perfectly legal. Help-wanted ads were divided into "Male" and "Female" sections, channeling women into low-paying jobs regardless of their qualifications. If she was raped by her husband, that was not a crime. If she was beaten, police were reluctant to intervene in "domestic matters." If she became pregnant against her will, abortion was illegal in most states.

By 1980, the landscape had transformed. The Equal Pay Act of 1963 prohibited wage discrimination based on sex. Title VII of the Civil Rights Act of 1964 banned employment discrimination on the basis of sex. The Equal Credit Opportunity Act of 1974 gave women the right to obtain credit in their own names. Roe v. Wade, decided in 1973, established a constitutional right to abortion. Women were entering the workforce, attending college, and entering professions that had been closed to them for generations.

This was the work of the second wave of feminism—a movement that emerged in the 1960s and transformed American society in ways that still reverberate today. Like the suffrage movement before it, the second wave faced fierce opposition from the Masculine Triad. And like the suffrage movement, its victories were real but incomplete, its gains always contested and sometimes reversed.

This chapter examines the second wave of feminism: its origins, its achievements, its opposition, and its ultimate fate. It is a story of how the Masculine Triad adapts to changing circumstances, deploying new arguments and new tactics while pursuing the same fundamental goal of maintaining male supremacy.

. . .

The Problem That Has No Name

In 1963, Betty Friedan published *The Feminine Mystique*, a book that gave voice to millions of women's unspoken dissatisfaction. Friedan had surveyed her fellow Smith College graduates and discovered that many of them—educated women who had been told that marriage and motherhood would bring fulfillment—were deeply unhappy. They suffered from what Friedan called "the problem that has no name."

The problem was not the absence of love or family or material comfort. The problem was the absence of identity. Women who had been raised to believe that their highest calling was to be wives and mothers found that this calling, however worthy, did not constitute a complete human life. They had been told that femininity was the ultimate goal, that they should find fulfillment in housework and child-rearing and serving their husbands. And many of them found that they could not.

"Each suburban wife struggled with it alone," Friedan
wrote. "As she made the beds, shopped for groceries,
matched slipcover material, ate peanut butter sandwiches
with her children, chauffeured Cub Scouts and Brownies,
lay beside her husband at night—she was afraid to ask
even of herself the silent question—'Is this all?'"

The Feminine Mystique was not the first feminist text of the twentieth century. Simone de Beauvoir's *The Second Sex* had been published in 1949, providing a philosophical foundation for understanding women's oppression. But Friedan's book reached ordinary American women in a way that de Beauvoir's had not. It became a bestseller, selling millions of copies and catalyzing a movement.

The book had its limitations. Friedan focused on educated, middle-class, white women—women who had the luxury of staying home while their husbands worked. Poor women, working-class women, Black women faced different problems: not the emptiness of enforced domesticity but the burden of working for low wages while still being expected to maintain homes and raise children. The feminine mystique was a problem primarily for women who could afford to be mystified.

But the book's impact was undeniable. It gave women permission to acknowledge their dissatisfaction, to name what they had been feeling, to demand more from life than domesticity alone could provide. And it helped launch a movement that would challenge the Masculine Triad on multiple fronts.

. . .

The Movement Takes Shape

The second wave of feminism emerged in the context of other social movements. The civil rights movement had demonstrated the power of collective action to challenge entrenched systems of oppression. The anti-war movement had mobilized millions of Americans, including many women, in political activism. The general ferment of the 1960s created space for challenging all kinds of established hierarchies—including the hierarchy of sex.

The National Organization for Women

In 1966, Betty Friedan joined with Pauli Murray, Aileen Hernandez, and others to found the National Organization for Women (NOW). The organization's founding was partly a response to the Equal Employment Opportunity Commission's (EEOC) failure to enforce the sex discrimination provisions of Title VII. The law had been passed, but the agency charged with enforcing it regarded sex discrimination as secondary to its "real" mission of addressing racial discrimination.

NOW's statement of purpose, written by Friedan, declared its intention "to bring women into full participation in the mainstream of American society now, exercising all the privileges and responsibilities thereof in truly equal partnership with men." The organization would become the largest feminist organization in America, with half a million members at its peak.

NOW represented what was called "liberal feminism"—the belief that women's equality could be achieved through legal reform, through ending discrimination in employment and education, through giving women the same opportunities that men enjoyed. Liberal feminists did not seek to overthrow capitalism or transform the fundamental structure of society; they sought to ensure that women could compete on equal terms within existing institutions.

Radical Feminism

Other feminists went further. Radical feminists argued that the oppression of women was not merely a matter of legal inequality but was built into the very structure of patriarchal society. They challenged not just employment discrimination but the institution of marriage itself, not just unequal pay but the sexual exploitation of women, not just workplace barriers but the fundamental relationship between men and women.

Radical feminists developed the practice of "consciousness-raising"—small group discussions in which women shared their experiences and came to understand that what they had thought were personal problems were actually political issues. The personal was political; the oppression women experienced in their daily lives was not individual misfortune but systematic subordination.

The radical wing of the movement challenged assumptions that liberal feminists often left unexamined. It asked why women did unpaid domestic labor while men were paid for their work. It asked why women were held responsible for controlling male sexuality while men faced no corresponding responsibility. It asked why violence against women was tolerated and even normalized.

Achievements

The second wave achieved remarkable legislative and legal victories. The Equal Pay Act of 1963 made it illegal to pay women less than men for equal work. Title VII of the Civil Rights Act of 1964 prohibited employment discrimination based on sex—although "sex" had been added to the bill almost as an afterthought, by a Southern congressman who hoped the addition would sink the entire legislation. Title IX of the Education Amendments of 1972 prohibited sex discrimination in educational institutions receiving federal funding, opening doors for women in athletics and academia.

The Equal Credit Opportunity Act of 1974 ended the practice of denying women credit cards and loans without male cosigners. Before this law, banks routinely refused to issue credit to women in their own names, regardless of their income or creditworthiness. A woman might be a successful professional, but without her husband's or father's signature, she could not get a mortgage or a credit card.

Roe v. Wade in 1973 established that the Constitution protected a woman's right to choose abortion, striking down state laws that had criminalized the procedure. This decision, more than any other, would become the focal point of conservative opposition to feminism—and the most vulnerable of the movement's achievements.

Beyond legislation, the movement changed cultural attitudes. Women entered professions that had been closed to them: law, medicine, business, academia. The percentage of women in the workforce rose steadily. Educational opportunities expanded. The assumption that women's place was in the home, while never entirely abandoned, lost its hegemonic grip on American culture.

• • •

Evidence for the Prosecution: GOD

The second wave of feminism faced opposition from religious institutions and ideological movements that provided justification for traditional gender roles. This opposition drew on both religious authority and emerging conservative political ideology.

Religious Opposition

Religious conservatives opposed feminism as an attack on divinely ordained gender roles. God had created men and women differently, with different natures and different purposes. Men were meant to lead; women were meant to follow. Men were meant to provide; women were meant to nurture. The feminist movement, in this view, was not merely misguided social policy but rebellion against God's design for human life.

The religious opposition was particularly mobilized around abortion. After Roe v. Wade, evangelical and Catholic churches organized to oppose what they called the "murder of the unborn." The anti-abortion movement—which would later rebrand itself as "pro-life"—drew heavily on religious rhetoric and religious networks. It framed the issue not as a matter of women's rights but as a matter of protecting innocent life, with women who sought abortions cast as either victims of a permissive culture or as selfish killers of their own children.

But the religious opposition extended beyond abortion. Conservative churches taught that women should submit to their husbands, that mothers should stay home with their children, that the feminist movement threatened the family structure that God had ordained. These teachings reached millions of Americans through Sunday sermons, religious broadcasting, and a growing network of religious schools and institutions.

The New Right

The 1970s saw the emergence of a "New Right" that combined religious conservatism with political organizing. This movement opposed feminism not merely on religious grounds but as part of a broader defense of "traditional values" against what it saw as the excesses of the 1960s. The New Right linked opposition to feminism with opposition to civil rights, to the counterculture, to everything that seemed to threaten the social order that had prevailed before the upheavals of the previous decade.

The New Right developed a sophisticated political operation, using direct mail, grassroots organizing, and media savvy to mobilize millions of voters. It found in feminism a perfect target: a movement that could be portrayed as attacking the family, as undermining traditional morality, as threatening the natural order. The feminist was caricatured as a bra-burning radical, a man-hater, a destroyer of homes and families.

GOD thus fulfilled his role in the opposition to second-wave feminism by providing religious justification (biblical teachings on women's submission and God's design for gender), moral framing (abortion as murder, feminism as attack on the family), and ideological infrastructure (the network of conservative churches, religious broadcasters, and Christian organizations that spread anti-feminist messages to millions).

• • •

Evidence for the Prosecution: THE DEVIL

While the second wave achieved significant legislative victories, the machinery of government also resisted and limited those victories. Laws were passed but not enforced. Rights were granted but not protected. And ultimately, the movement's most ambitious goal—the Equal Rights Amendment—was defeated.

Enforcement Failures

The passage of anti-discrimination laws did not automatically end discrimination. The EEOC, tasked with enforcing Title VII, initially regarded sex discrimination as a joke. The agency had little will and limited authority to enforce the law's sex-based provisions. EEOC officials noted that there was "virtually no legislative history explaining Congress's intent in outlawing sex discrimination"—since the provision had been added as a poison pill designed to kill the entire bill.

The practical effect was that sex discrimination continued even after it became illegal. Help-wanted ads continued to be divided by sex until NOW's persistent lobbying forced the EEOC to address the issue in 1973. Women continued to be paid less than men, denied promotions, subjected to harassment, and fired for becoming pregnant.

The law was on the books, but enforcement was sporadic at best.

Similarly, Executive Order 11246, signed by President Johnson in 1965 to prohibit discrimination by federal contractors, originally omitted sex. It took sustained pressure from women's organizations to get sex added to the order in 1967. Even after the addition, enforcement was weak. The machinery of government moved slowly when it moved at all.

The ERA Defeat

The Equal Rights Amendment was the feminist movement's most ambitious legislative goal. The amendment, first proposed in 1923, stated simply: "Equality of rights under the law shall not be denied or abridged by the United States or by any State on account of sex."

In 1972, the amendment seemed destined for ratification. Congress passed it overwhelmingly, with only twenty-four votes against it in the House and eight in the Senate. Within a year, thirty states had ratified it, leaving it only eight states short of the thirty-eight needed for adoption. Supporters expected quick ratification.

But then momentum stalled. By 1977, only thirty-five states had ratified. Congress extended the ratification deadline from 1979 to 1982, but no additional states ratified. Five states that had ratified actually rescinded their ratifications. When the deadline arrived on June 30, 1982, the ERA was dead, three states short of adoption.

The amendment's defeat resulted from a combination of factors: growing conservative opposition, the rise of the New Right, divisions within the feminist movement itself. But at its core, it reflected the continued resistance of political institutions to enshrining women's equality in the Constitution. The same Congress that had passed the amendment overwhelmingly allowed it to die without taking action to revive it. State legislatures that had initially supported it reversed course or refused to vote.

THE DEVIL thus fulfilled his role in the opposition to second-wave feminism through enforcement failures (weak implementation of anti-discrimination laws, particularly in the early years), institutional resistance (the defeat of the ERA despite overwhelming initial support), and political retreat (the removal of ERA support from the Republican platform in 1980, signaling that women's constitutional equality was no longer a bipartisan goal).

• • •

Evidence for the Prosecution: MAN

Individual men benefited from the continued subordination of women and organized to maintain those benefits. But the most effective opposition to second-wave feminism came from an unexpected source: a woman who mobilized other women against their own equality.

Phyllis Schlafly and STOP ERA

Phyllis Schlafly was a lawyer, author, and conservative activist who had made her name in the anticommunist movement of the 1950s and 1960s. In 1972, she launched a campaign against the Equal Rights Amendment that would prove devastatingly effective.

Schlafly's STOP ERA campaign—"STOP" stood for "Stop Taking Our Privileges"—argued that the ERA would harm women rather than help them. She claimed it would subject women to the military draft, eliminate laws protecting women in divorce and custody cases, require unisex bathrooms, and lead to abortion on demand. Many of these claims were exaggerated or false, but they were effective.

Schlafly understood something that ERA supporters often missed: not all women wanted equality as feminists defined it. Many women had built their lives around traditional gender roles—as wives, mothers, homemakers—and saw feminism as an attack on those roles. They did not want to be told that their choices were inferior or that their lives were unfulfilled. Schlafly gave them a voice and a movement.

"What I am defending is the real rights of women," Schlafly said. "A woman should have the right to be in the home as a wife and mother." She opened her speeches with quips like "I'd like to thank my husband for letting me be here tonight"—statements that infuriated feminists but delighted her supporters. She and her followers brought homemade bread and apple pies to state legislators, with slogans like "Preserve us from a congressional jam; Vote against the ERA sham."

The irony was rich. Schlafly herself was a highly educated professional woman who traveled constantly, gave speeches, wrote books, ran organizations, and competed in the male-dominated world of politics. She was, in many ways, a living refutation of the traditional gender roles she championed. But her personal choices did not prevent her from arguing that other women should be confined to domesticity.

Women Against Women

The anti-ERA movement revealed a painful truth: women did not automatically support women's equality. Many women had internalized the ideology of separate spheres and genuinely believed that traditional gender roles were natural, beneficial, and divinely ordained. They feared that equality would mean the loss of protections they valued—the husband's obligation to support his wife, the mother's presumptive right to custody, the exemption from military service.

Schlafly was able to mobilize these women in ways that male anti-feminists could not. A man arguing against women's equality could be dismissed as self-interested; a woman making the same arguments seemed to prove that feminism was not what women really wanted. The anti-ERA movement was led by women, staffed by women, and its arguments were shaped by women's fears and concerns.

This was not entirely new. The anti-suffrage movement had also been led in part by women. Women have always been divided on questions of gender equality, and some have always been willing to defend systems that subordinate them. They do so for various reasons: religious conviction, genuine belief in traditional roles, fear of change, or calculation that they benefit more from the current system than they would from equality.

The Benefits of Subordination

Men continued to benefit from women's subordination even as that subordination diminished. Women's entry into the workforce meant competition for jobs that men had previously monopolized. Women's demands for equal pay meant that employers could no longer extract cheap female labor. Women's reproductive rights meant that men could no longer control women's fertility as they once had.

Many men resisted these changes, sometimes openly and sometimes through subtler forms of discrimination and harassment. Workplaces remained hostile to women even after laws prohibited discrimination. Sexual harassment was pervasive and largely unpunished. The "glass ceiling" prevented women from rising to top positions even when they had the qualifications and experience.

MAN thus fulfilled his role in the opposition to second-wave feminism through continued discrimination (workplace barriers, harassment, unequal pay despite legal prohibitions), political opposition (male legislators who voted against women's rights or failed to enforce laws protecting them), and mobilization of women (using female anti-feminists like Schlafly to give the opposition a face that was harder to dismiss as mere male self-interest).

* * *

The Movement's Limits

The second wave of feminism achieved remarkable victories, but it also had significant limitations—limitations that would shape feminist politics for generations to come.

Race and Class

The movement was dominated by white, middle-class women whose concerns did not always align with those of poor women or women of color. The "problem that has no name" was a problem primarily for women who could afford to stay home; poor women had always worked, and their problem was not the emptiness of enforced domesticity but the burden of labor without adequate compensation or support.

Black women faced the intersection of racism and sexism—what would later be called "intersectionality." They were often excluded from feminist organizations or found that their concerns were marginalized within them. The mainstream women's movement focused on issues like breaking into corporate management or achieving equal pay in professional jobs, while ignoring the struggles of domestic workers, factory workers, and women in the informal economy.

This limitation was not merely a failure of inclusion; it was a failure of analysis. A feminism that focused only on removing barriers to individual achievement could not address the structural inequalities that kept most women subordinated regardless of their individual talents or ambitions. Opening the doors to the corporate boardroom did little for women who would never be anywhere near those doors.

The Backlash

By the late 1970s, the feminist movement faced a growing backlash. The New Right had mobilized, the ERA had stalled, and conservative politicians were winning elections by running against feminism and other movements of the 1960s. Ronald Reagan's election in 1980 signaled a new era in which feminist gains would be contested and sometimes reversed.

The backlash was partly a response to the movement's real achievements. Because feminism had changed things—had opened doors, shifted attitudes, transformed expectations—it generated opposition from those who preferred the old order. The very success of the movement created the conditions for its opposition.

But the backlash was also facilitated by the movement's own divisions. Feminists disagreed among themselves about pornography, about sexuality, about the relationship between feminism and other social movements. These disagreements weakened the movement's political effectiveness and made it easier for opponents to exploit divisions.

• • •

The Masculine Triad Adapts

The second wave of feminism forced the Masculine Triad to adapt. The old arguments for women's subordination—that women were naturally inferior, that they belonged in the home, that they were unfit for public life—had lost much of their persuasive power. New arguments were needed.

The Triad found those arguments in the defense of "traditional values," in the protection of the "family," in the claim that feminism harmed women rather than helped them. These arguments accepted the premise that women's interests mattered while denying that feminism served those interests. They portrayed feminists as the real oppressors—of homemakers who chose traditional roles, of unborn children, of the family itself.

This was a sophisticated adaptation. Rather than openly defending male supremacy, the Triad defended "natural" differences between the sexes, "traditional" family structures, and women's "right" to be wives and mothers. It co-opted the language of rights and choice while using that language to limit women's actual choices.

The adaptation was also institutional. The Republican Party, which had supported the ERA since 1940, removed that support from its platform in 1980. Conservative legal organizations formed to challenge feminist gains in the courts. Think tanks produced studies purporting to show that feminist policies harmed women and families. A network of conservative media outlets spread anti-feminist messages to millions.

The second wave had won many battles, but the war continued. The Masculine Triad had been forced to retreat, but it had not surrendered. It had adapted, regrouped, and prepared for a counteroffensive that would intensify in the decades to come. The question was not whether women had made progress—they clearly had —but whether that progress could be sustained against a backlash that was only beginning to gather force.

CHAPTER FIFTEEN

The Battle for Bodily Autonomy

The evidence in this chapter demonstrates the Masculine Triad's central battleground: control of women's bodies. Here the prosecution will show that reproductive rights are not merely a political issue but the fundamental question of whether women own themselves or are owned by others.

On June 24, 2022, the Supreme Court of the United States issued its decision in Dobbs v. Jackson Women's Health Organization. By a vote of 6-3, the Court overturned Roe v. Wade, eliminating the constitutional right to abortion that had stood for nearly fifty years. For the first time in American history, the Supreme Court had taken away a fundamental right.

The decision was not unexpected. For decades, opponents of abortion rights had worked to pack the courts with judges hostile to Roe. Three of the justices in the Dobbs majority had been appointed by a single president. Two of them had been confirmed by a Senate that represented a minority of the American population. And all five of the majority's male justices had been appointed by presidents who lost the popular vote.

Within weeks of the decision, abortion became illegal or severely restricted in roughly half the states. Clinics closed. Women with dangerous pregnancies were denied care. Doctors faced criminal prosecution for providing medical treatment. The consequences were immediate and devastating—and they fell most heavily on poor women and women of color, who lacked the resources to travel to states where abortion remained legal.

The Dobbs decision represents the most dramatic recent victory of the Masculine Triad in its ongoing effort to control women's bodies. But it is only the latest chapter in a battle that has been waged for over a century—a battle over whether women have the right to determine what happens to their own bodies, or whether that right belongs to God, the state, and men.

• • •

The Comstock Era

In 1873, Congress passed a law that would shape American reproductive politics for nearly a century. Championed by Anthony Comstock, a Civil War veteran and anti-vice crusader, the Comstock Act criminalized the distribution of "obscene" materials through the mail. The law's definition of obscenity was broad enough to include not just pornography but any information about contraception or abortion. It became a federal crime to mail birth control devices, to send letters containing information about preventing pregnancy, or to advertise any product or service related to family planning.

Comstock himself was appointed as a special agent of the Post Office, empowered to enforce the law he had created. For the next four decades, he pursued his crusade against "obscenity" with zealous energy, arresting doctors, pharmacists, and anyone else who dared to provide women with information about controlling their fertility. Twenty-four states passed their own "little Comstock" laws, some even more restrictive than the federal statute.

The Comstock laws were not merely about obscenity; they were about control. They ensured that women could not access the information or technology that would allow them to decide when and whether to bear children. A woman's fertility was not her own to manage. It belonged to her husband, to the state, to God—to anyone but herself.

Margaret Sanger's Challenge

The woman who did more than anyone else to challenge the Comstock regime was Margaret Sanger, a nurse who had witnessed firsthand the consequences of uncontrolled fertility. Working among poor immigrant women on New York's Lower East Side, Sanger saw women destroy their health through repeated pregnancies and die from botched back-alley abortions. She watched her own mother, who had borne eleven children and suffered seven miscarriages, waste away and die at fifty.

In 1914, Sanger coined the term "birth control" and began openly defying the Comstock laws. She distributed information about contraception, knowing it would lead to her arrest. She fled to Europe to avoid prosecution, returned to face trial, and was eventually jailed. But she never stopped fighting.

In 1916, Sanger opened the first birth control clinic in America, in Brooklyn, New York. It was shut down within ten days. She opened another. It too was shut down. She founded what would become Planned Parenthood. She lobbied, organized, and agitated for decades, always with the same goal: to give women control over their own fertility.

Sanger's legacy is complicated. She associated with eugenicists and made statements that were racist and classist. Her movement focused primarily on married women and often excluded poor women and women of color from its benefits. But her fundamental insight—that women could not be free unless they could control their own reproduction—remains central to the struggle for women's rights.

• • •

The Right to Privacy

The constitutional breakthrough came in 1965, with Griswold v. Connecticut. The case challenged a Connecticut law, dating from 1879, that made it a crime to use "any drug, medicinal article, or instrument for the purpose of preventing conception." The law was rarely enforced, but it was still on the books—and it prevented organizations like Planned Parenthood from openly providing contraceptive services.

Estelle Griswold, executive director of the Planned Parenthood League of Connecticut, decided to force a test case. She opened a birth control clinic in New Haven, openly provided contraceptives to married couples, and waited to be arrested. Within ten days, she was. Convicted and fined, she appealed her case all the way to the Supreme Court.

In a 7-2 decision, the Court struck down Connecticut's law. Justice William O. Douglas, writing for the majority, found that the Constitution protects a "right to marital privacy" that includes the right to use contraception. Although no such right is explicitly mentioned in the Constitution's text, Douglas found it within the "penumbras" and "emanations" of other constitutional provisions—the First Amendment's protection of association, the Third Amendment's prohibition on quartering soldiers, the Fourth Amendment's protection against unreasonable searches, and the Fifth Amendment's protection against self-incrimination.

Griswold was revolutionary. For the first time, the Court recognized that the Constitution protects intimate decisions—decisions about marriage, family, and reproduction—from government interference. This right to privacy would become the constitutional foundation for later decisions protecting contraception for unmarried individuals (Eisenstadt v. Baird, 1972), abortion (Roe v. Wade, 1973),

• • •

Roe and Its Aftermath

In 1973, the Supreme Court decided Roe v. Wade, striking down a Texas law that criminalized abortion except to save the mother's life. The Court held that the constitutional right to privacy "is broad enough to encompass a woman's decision whether or not to terminate her pregnancy."

Roe established a framework for balancing a woman's right to choose against the state's interests in protecting maternal health and potential life. During the first trimester, the decision to abort was left entirely to the woman and her physician. During the second trimester, states could regulate abortion to protect maternal health. During the third trimester, after fetal viability, states could prohibit abortion entirely—except where necessary to preserve the woman's life or health.

The decision was transformative. At the time Roe was decided, abortion was illegal in most states. Women seeking abortions had to travel to the few states where it was legal, seek out illegal providers, or attempt to induce abortions themselves. The consequences were predictable: thousands of women were injured or killed by unsafe abortions. After Roe, abortion became far safer and more accessible, though significant barriers remained for poor women and women in rural areas.

The Counterattack

The opposition to Roe was immediate and sustained. Religious conservatives, particularly evangelical Christians and Catholics, mobilized against what they called "abortion on demand." The Republican Party, which had previously supported abortion rights, gradually adopted an anti-abortion platform. A well-funded movement emerged, dedicated to overturning Roe through litigation, legislation, and political action.

States passed hundreds of laws designed to make abortion as difficult as possible without technically violating Roe. Waiting periods required women to make multiple trips to clinics. Mandatory counseling laws forced doctors to provide information designed to discourage abortion. Parental consent and notification laws created barriers for minors. Targeted restrictions on abortion providers (TRAP laws) imposed onerous requirements on clinics, forcing many to close. And the Hyde Amendment, passed in 1976, prohibited federal funding for abortion, ensuring that poor women on Medicaid could not access the same services available to wealthier women.

In 1992, Planned Parenthood v. Casey reaffirmed Roe's "central holding" that women have a constitutional right to abortion before viability. But Casey also weakened Roe's protections, abandoning the trimester framework in favor of an "undue burden" standard that gave states more latitude to restrict abortion. Under Casey, states could regulate abortion as long as their regulations did not place a "substantial obstacle" in the path of a woman seeking an abortion.

The result was a slow erosion of abortion access. Clinics closed. Waiting periods lengthened. The number of abortion providers declined. By the time Dobbs was decided, abortion was already effectively unavailable in many parts of the country, even though it remained technically legal.

• • •

Evidence for the Prosecution: GOD

The opposition to reproductive rights has always drawn heavily on religious authority. The arguments are familiar: life begins at conception; abortion is murder; God's design for women is motherhood; contraception interferes with divine providence. These religious claims provide ideological justification for restricting women's bodily autonomy.

The Religious Coalition

The anti-abortion movement brought together religious groups that had previously had little in common. Evangelical Protestants, who had traditionally viewed abortion as a "Catholic issue," joined forces with Catholics in opposing Roe. Mormons, Orthodox Jews, and other religious conservatives added their voices. This coalition, united by opposition to abortion, became a powerful political force.

The religious framing of abortion as "murder" transformed the debate. If abortion is murder, then no compromise is possible. If a fetus is a person with full moral status from the moment of conception, then the woman's rights become secondary to the fetus's right to life. The religious framework leaves no room for considering the woman's health, her circumstances, her autonomy, or her judgment. She becomes merely a vessel for the fetus, her body subordinated to its needs.

Science as Cover

As in earlier eras, religious arguments have been supplemented with claims dressed in scientific language. Anti-abortion advocates promote the concept of "fetal pain" at early gestational ages, despite the absence of scientific evidence for pain perception before the third trimester. They claim that abortion causes breast cancer, despite the consensus of medical research to the contrary. They argue that "abortion reversal" is possible after taking the first of two medication abortion pills, despite the lack of scientific support for this claim.

These pseudo-scientific arguments serve to obscure the religious foundations of anti-abortion politics. By claiming scientific authority, opponents of abortion can present their position as based on objective facts rather than religious doctrine—even though the scientific establishment overwhelmingly supports abortion rights and access.

GOD thus fulfills his role in the opposition to reproductive rights by providing religious justification (life begins at conception, abortion is murder, God's design requires motherhood), moral absolutism (no compromise is possible when "life" is at stake), and pseudo-scientific cover (claims about fetal pain, abortion and breast cancer, and other medically discredited assertions that give religious arguments a scientific veneer).

• • •

Evidence for the Prosecution: THE DEVIL

The machinery of government has been the primary instrument for restricting reproductive rights. Legislatures pass laws limiting abortion. Courts uphold those laws or strike down protections. Prosecutors pursue criminal charges against women and providers.

The state's coercive power is deployed to control women's bodies.

The Legislative Assault

Between Roe and Dobbs, states passed over a thousand laws restricting abortion. These laws took many forms: gestational limits prohibiting abortion after a certain number of weeks; mandatory waiting periods requiring multiple clinic visits; counseling requirements forcing doctors to provide medically inaccurate information; TRAP laws imposing unnecessary requirements on clinics; bans on specific procedures; and requirements for parental involvement when minors seek abortions.

The cumulative effect was devastating. In some states, only a single clinic remained to serve an entire population. Women had to travel hundreds of miles, take time off work, arrange childcare, and find money for travel and lodging—all to exercise a constitutional right. For poor women, rural women, and women with inflexible work schedules, these barriers were often insurmountable.

The Judicial Strategy

The anti-abortion movement understood that Roe could only be overturned by changing the composition of the Supreme Court. For decades, they worked to ensure that Republican presidents nominated justices hostile to abortion rights and that the Senate confirmed them. They created organizations to identify, cultivate, and promote conservative judges. They made judicial appointments a litmus test for Republican candidates.

The strategy succeeded. Between 2017 and 2020, three new justices—Neil Gorsuch, Brett Kavanaugh, and Amy Coney Barrett—joined the Court, all appointed by President Trump, all with records suggesting hostility to abortion rights. Barrett was confirmed just days before the 2020 election to replace Ruth Bader Ginsburg, whose dying wish was that she not be replaced until after the election.

Within two years of Barrett's confirmation, Roe was overturned.

The Dobbs Aftermath

The consequences of Dobbs have been swift and severe. Roughly half the states have banned or severely restricted abortion. Clinics have closed. Doctors have fled states where they face criminal prosecution for providing care. Women with dangerous pregnancies—ectopic pregnancies, miscarriages requiring intervention, pregnancies with fatal fetal anomalies—have been denied treatment because doctors fear prosecution.

The horror stories have accumulated. A woman in Texas with a non-viable pregnancy developed sepsis because doctors delayed treatment until she was near death. A woman in Ohio, pregnant from rape at ten years old, had to travel to Indiana for an abortion. A woman in Louisiana was forced to carry a fetus with no skull to term because her state's law offered no exception for fatal fetal anomalies.

Research has documented the consequences: increases in maternal mortality and morbidity, especially among Black women; increases in infant mortality, especially among Black infants; doctors leaving states with abortion bans; medical students avoiding residencies in those states; and widespread confusion among healthcare providers about what care they can legally provide.

THE DEVIL thus fulfills his role in the opposition to reproductive rights through legislative restriction (hundreds of laws making abortion difficult or impossible to access), judicial capture (a decades-long strategy to install anti-abortion judges culminating in Dobbs), and medical harm (increased maternal and infant mortality, delayed care for pregnancy complications, and the exodus of healthcare providers from ban states).

• • •

Evidence for the Prosecution: MAN

The opposition to reproductive rights is overwhelmingly driven by men. Men wrote the Comstock laws. Men wrote the state laws that criminalized abortion before Roe. Men constitute the majority of state legislators who have passed abortion restrictions since Roe. Men constitute the majority of the Supreme Court that overturned Roe. And men have obvious interests in controlling women's reproduction.

The Male Interest

Control over reproduction is control over women's lives. A woman who cannot control her fertility cannot control her education, her career, her economic prospects, or her relationships. She is subject to the biological consequences of male sexual activity in ways that men are not. Pregnancy, childbirth, and child-rearing impose burdens on women that do not fall on men—unless women can choose when and whether to bear children.

The Supreme Court recognized this in Planned Parenthood v. Casey: "The ability of women to participate equally in the economic and social life of the Nation has been facilitated by their ability to control their reproductive lives." Control over reproduction is not merely a medical matter; it is a precondition for women's equality.

Men who oppose reproductive rights may do so for various reasons: religious conviction, political calculation, or simple misogyny. But whatever their stated reasons, the effect is the same: women are denied control over their own bodies, their own futures, their own lives. And men retain the power to determine when and whether women bear children.

The Gender of Power

The Dobbs decision was written by Justice Samuel Alito and joined by four other male justices: Clarence Thomas, Neil Gorsuch, Brett Kavanaugh, and (in the judgment only) Chief Justice John Roberts. Justice Amy Coney Barrett, the only woman in the majority, joined Alito's opinion. But the driving force behind the decision was male.

In his concurrence, Justice Thomas went further than the majority, arguing that the Court should reconsider other decisions grounded in the right to privacy—including decisions protecting contraception. The suggestion that Griswold might be overturned reveals how far the assault on reproductive rights might extend. It is not merely abortion that is at stake; it is the entire framework of constitutional privacy that has protected intimate decisions from government interference.

MAN thus fulfills his role in the opposition to reproductive rights through direct control (men constitute the majority of legislators and judges restricting reproductive rights), indirect benefit (control over reproduction ensures women's subordination), and ideological justification (male religious and political leaders provide the arguments for restricting women's bodily autonomy).

. . .

The Stakes

The battle over reproductive rights is not merely about abortion. It is about the fundamental question of whether women are persons with full bodily autonomy or vessels whose primary purpose is reproduction.

If women have bodily autonomy, they can decide when and whether to bear children. They can pursue education and careers without the constant risk of unwanted pregnancy derailing their plans. They can choose their sexual partners and the terms of their relationships without being permanently bound by the biological consequences of those choices. They can be full participants in economic, social, and political life.

If women do not have bodily autonomy—if their reproductive functions can be controlled by the state, by religion, by men—then they cannot be fully free. They are subject to a form of subordination that has no male equivalent. No one forces men to carry pregnancies to term against their will. No one criminalizes men's reproductive decisions. The asymmetry is total.

The Masculine Triad understands these stakes, which is why reproductive rights have been so fiercely contested. Every advance—the end of Comstock, Griswold, Roe—has been met with fierce resistance. And when that resistance succeeds, as it did in Dobbs, the consequences for women are immediate and severe.

The battle continues. Since Dobbs, voters in several states have passed ballot measures protecting abortion rights, sometimes in deep-red states where such results seemed impossible. The political backlash against abortion bans has been significant. But in other states, restrictions have tightened, prosecutions have increased, and women have suffered and died.

This is what control of the female body looks like in practice. Not ancient history but contemporary reality. Not abstract ideology but concrete suffering. The Masculine Triad adapts, retreats, advances, but never abandons its fundamental project: to ensure that women's bodies remain subject to control by forces other than the women who inhabit them.

CHAPTER SIXTEEN

The Politics of Sexual Violence

The prosecution now presents evidence of the Masculine Triad's role in sexual violence—not merely individual acts, but the systematic legal, religious, and social structures that have protected perpetrators and punished victims throughout history. The evidence will demonstrate that violence against women is not an aberration but an enforcement mechanism.

In October 1991, a law professor named Anita Hill testified before the United States Senate Judiciary Committee. She had been called to address allegations that Clarence Thomas, then a nominee for the Supreme Court, had sexually harassed her when she worked for him at the Department of Education and the Equal Employment Opportunity Commission. Before an all-white, all-male committee, Hill described how Thomas had repeatedly asked her out, discussed pornography in graphic detail, and made sexual comments about her appearance.

The senators' response was revealing. They questioned Hill's credibility, asked whether she was a "scorned woman," suggested she had invented the allegations for political reasons, and subjected her to hours of hostile interrogation about matters that should never have been in question. Thomas denied everything and characterized the hearings as "a high-tech lynching." The Senate confirmed him by a vote of 52-48. He remains on the Supreme Court today.

The Hill-Thomas hearings were a watershed moment. For the first time, millions of Americans watched a woman describe workplace sexual harassment on national television. Many women recognized their own experiences in Hill's testimony—the unwanted advances, the graphic comments, the power differential that made resistance dangerous. And they recognized, too, the response: disbelief, blame, character assassination, and ultimately, the elevation of the accused to the highest court in the land.

Sexual violence has always been political. Who can be violated, by whom, under what circumstances, and with what consequences—these questions are determined not by nature but by law, custom, and power. For most of human history, the answers have been structured to protect male prerogatives and to deny women recourse. This chapter examines how the Masculine Triad has operated in the realm of sexual violence, and how women have fought to change the rules.

• • •

Rape as Property Crime

The earliest recorded laws on rape treated it not as a crime against the woman but as a crime against the men who owned her. The Code of Hammurabi, one of the oldest surviving legal codes, classified the rape of a virgin as property damage against her father. The woman herself had no standing; she was merely the damaged property. If a man raped another man's wife, both the rapist and the victim were to be killed—a punishment that makes sense only if the crime is understood as an offense against the husband's property rights in his wife's sexuality.

This conception of rape as a property crime persisted for millennia. In medieval Europe, rape laws existed primarily to protect the interests of fathers and husbands in women's virginity and fidelity. The rape of an unmarried woman was compensable with money paid to her father; the rape of a married woman was an offense against her husband. The woman's own experience—her trauma, her violation, her autonomy—was legally irrelevant.

The word "rape" itself derives from the Latin *rapere*, meaning "to seize" or "to carry off." The term originally referred to the abduction of women, not to sexual violence per se. A man who "raped" a woman took her from the possession of another man. The sexual violation was incidental; the theft was the crime.

The Common Law Inheritance

English common law, which formed the basis for American law, carried forward many of these assumptions. Sir Matthew Hale, the seventeenth-century jurist whose influence on Anglo-American law was enormous, articulated several principles that would shape rape law for centuries.

First, Hale established the marital rape exemption. A husband, he declared, could not be guilty of raping his wife, because marriage constituted permanent consent that could not be retracted. Once a woman married, her body became her husband's to use as he wished. This principle remained law in most American states until the 1970s.

Second, Hale established the principle that rape accusations should be viewed with special skepticism. "Rape is an accusation easily to be made and hard to be proved, and harder to be defended by the party accused, tho never so innocent." This instruction—that juries should be especially cautious in believing women who claimed to have been raped—was given in American courts into the late twentieth century.

Third, Hale established that a woman's sexual history was relevant to her credibility. If she had consented to sex before, with anyone, she was less likely to be believed when she claimed non-consent. This assumption—that unchaste women were both more likely to consent and more likely to lie—was embedded in the law until rape shield statutes began to change it in the 1970s.

•••

The Burden of Proof

Under traditional rape law, the burden fell almost entirely on the victim. She had to prove not only that intercourse occurred but that she had not consented—and that she had actively resisted. The resistance requirement was extraordinary. In some states, the legal standard was that the victim must have resisted "to the utmost." A 1906 Wisconsin Supreme Court decision reversed a rape conviction because the victim had "only" struggled and screamed; the court held that "there must be the most vehement exercise of every physical means or faculty within the woman's power to resist the penetration of her person."

This requirement had no parallel in other crimes. Robbery victims were not required to fight their attackers "to the utmost" before the law would recognize that they had been robbed. Assault victims did not have to prove that they had physically resisted their assailants. Only rape victims were required to risk serious injury or death by fighting back, and only then would the law consider their claims credible.

The resistance requirement reflected deep assumptions about women and sex. It assumed that women secretly wanted sex and would falsely cry rape afterward. It assumed that a "real" rape victim would fight to the death rather than submit. And it protected men by ensuring that most rapes—those accomplished through intimidation, coercion, or the victim's reasonable fear of violence—could not be prosecuted.

Corroboration and Character

Many states also required corroboration: evidence beyond the victim's testimony to prove that a rape had occurred. Unlike with other crimes, the victim's word was not enough. There had to be witnesses, physical evidence, or other independent proof. Given that most rapes occur in private and leave limited physical evidence, this requirement made prosecution nearly impossible in many cases.

Even when cases went to trial, defense attorneys were permitted—indeed, encouraged—to attack the victim's sexual history. The assumption was that a woman who had consented to sex before was more likely to have consented this time, and more likely to lie about it afterward. A victim's entire sexual past could be paraded before the jury to discredit her. The humiliation and violation of having one's intimate life exposed in court deterred many women from reporting rape at all.

The legal system treated rape victims not as victims but as suspects. They entered the courtroom addressed as witnesses, not as complainants. They were interrogated about their clothing, their behavior, their previous relationships, their decision-making on the night in question. The implicit question was always: What did she do to deserve this? What did she do to invite it? The burden was on her to prove her innocence—to prove that she had not secretly wanted what was done to her.

• • •

Marital Rape and Permanent Consent

Nowhere was male sexual entitlement more explicitly encoded in law than in the marital rape exemption. Under the common law rule articulated by Sir Matthew Hale, a husband could not rape his wife because marriage constituted irrevocable consent to sex. A woman who married gave her husband permanent access to her body. She could not withdraw that consent; her refusal was legally meaningless.

This was not merely a legal technicality. It meant that a husband could force sex on his wife through violence, intimidation, or coercion, and the law would not recognize any crime. A man who raped a stranger could be imprisoned; a man who raped his wife had committed no offense. The law explicitly sanctioned sexual violence within marriage.

The marital rape exemption remained law in every American state until the mid-1970s. South Dakota briefly criminalized marital rape in 1975, then decriminalized it two years later. Nebraska eliminated the spousal exemption in 1975. But progress was slow. As late as 1993, marital rape was not a crime in all fifty states. And even after formal criminalization, many states retained distinctions between marital rape and other rape—requiring greater force, shorter reporting periods, or lesser penalties when the rapist was the victim's husband.

The arguments against criminalizing marital rape were revealing. Opponents claimed that criminalizing marital rape would destroy marriages, that wives would make false accusations, that the state had no business interfering in the marital bedroom. These arguments assumed that men had a right to sex from their wives regardless of the wives' consent—that marriage was, in essence, a license for sexual access.

Even today, legal loopholes persist. In some states, a husband who rapes his wife while she is unconscious, drugged, or incapacitated may face lesser charges or no charges at all. The law still treats marital rape as somehow less serious than "real" rape—as though a wife's body belongs to her husband in ways that a stranger's body does not.

• • •

Sexual Harassment and the Workplace

The concept of sexual harassment is remarkably recent. The term itself was coined in 1975 by a group of women at Cornell University who were trying to name experiences that had no legal recognition. Women had always been subjected to unwanted sexual attention at work— groping, propositions, graphic comments, demands for sex as a condition of employment—but until the 1970s, there was no word for it and no legal recourse against it.

Title VII of the Civil Rights Act of 1964 prohibited employment discrimination based on sex, but it was not clear that this prohibition extended to sexual harassment. The EEOC, the agency charged with enforcing Title VII, initially treated sex discrimination as a joke—a distraction from the "real" issue of racial discrimination. Claims of harassment were dismissed or ignored.

Through the 1970s, feminist lawyers and activists argued that sexual harassment was a form of sex discrimination. If women were subjected to conditions at work—demands for sex, hostile environments, constant sexual attention—that men were not subjected to, this was discrimination based on sex. A series of court cases in the late 1970s began to accept this argument, and in 1980, the EEOC issued guidelines recognizing sexual harassment as a violation of Title VII.

In 1986, the Supreme Court decided Meritor Savings Bank v. Vinson, affirming that sexual harassment violates Title VII. The case involved Mechelle Vinson, a bank employee whose supervisor had coerced her into sex dozens of times, in the bank vault, in the basement, wherever he could find her alone. The Court held that such conduct created a "hostile work environment" that constituted illegal discrimination.

The Anita Hill Moment

Despite these legal developments, sexual harassment remained widely tolerated and little understood. The 1991 Hill-Thomas hearings changed that. For the first time, millions of Americans heard a woman describe workplace harassment in detail—the graphic sexual comments, the unwanted attention, the pressure from a powerful supervisor.

The immediate aftermath was discouraging. Thomas was confirmed; Hill was vilified. She received death threats and was sent human feces in the mail. Conservative commentators attacked her credibility, her motives, her sanity. A sitting senator called her testimony "flat-out perjury."

But the longer-term effects were profound. Sexual harassment complaints filed with the EEOC more than doubled in the years following Hill's testimony. Congress passed the Civil Rights Act of 1991, giving victims of workplace harassment more legal recourse. Employers began implementing anti-harassment policies and training programs. And the issue entered public consciousness in a way it never had before.

Anita Hill did not defeat Clarence Thomas. But she made it possible for millions of women to name what had happened to them, to understand it as wrong, and to know they were not alone.

· · ·

Evidence for the Prosecution: GOD

Religious and ideological frameworks have consistently been used to justify male sexual entitlement and to blame women for sexual violence. The arguments vary, but the effect is the same: to place responsibility on women rather than on the men who assault them.

Eve's Daughters

The Christian tradition has long associated women with temptation and sin. Eve tempted Adam; women tempt men. This framework casts women as the source of male sexual desire and thus responsible for controlling it. If a man is aroused, it is because a woman aroused him. If he acts on that arousal, she bears some measure of blame.

This logic appears in religious teachings about modesty. Women are told to cover themselves, to avoid provocative clothing, to refrain from behaviors that might "tempt" men. The implication is that male sexual aggression is a natural response to female provocation—that men cannot be expected to control themselves in the face of exposed flesh. Women's bodies become dangerous objects that must be concealed for the protection of men.

Similar logic appears in secular form. What was she wearing? Had she been drinking? Why did she go to his room? These questions, asked of rape victims by police and prosecutors and defense attorneys and juries, assume that women's behavior determines whether they will be assaulted. They shift responsibility from the rapist to the victim. They treat sexual violence not as a choice made by the perpetrator but as a consequence invited by the victim.

Natural Male Sexuality

Another ideological justification frames male sexual aggression as natural and inevitable. Men, it is claimed, have stronger sex drives than women. They are biologically programmed to pursue sex aggressively. Expecting them to respect women's refusals is expecting them to fight their nature.

This naturalization of male aggression serves to excuse sexual violence. "Boys will be boys." "Men have needs." "What did she expect?" These phrases locate the cause of sexual violence in unchangeable male biology rather than in choices made by individual men. They suggest that the solution lies not in changing male behavior but in women protecting themselves from inevitable male aggression.

GOD thus fulfills his role in the politics of sexual violence by providing religious justification (women as temptresses responsible for male desire), moral frameworks that blame victims (modesty requirements, questions about behavior and clothing), and naturalization of male aggression (biological inevitability arguments that excuse rather than condemn).

• • •

Evidence for the Prosecution: THE DEVIL

The machinery of the state—law enforcement, the courts, the legislature—has historically failed to protect women from sexual violence and has often actively protected their abusers.

Laws That Protected Rapists

For most of American history, rape laws were structured to make conviction nearly impossible. The resistance requirement meant that women who submitted out of fear rather than fighting to the death could not prove rape. The corroboration requirement meant that private rapes—which is to say, most rapes—could not be prosecuted. The marital exemption meant that husbands could rape with impunity. The admissibility of sexual history meant that any woman who had ever had sex could be discredited.

These were not accidental gaps in the law. They were deliberate structures that protected men from accountability for sexual violence. Legislators—overwhelmingly male—wrote these laws. Judges—overwhelmingly male—interpreted them. The criminal justice system was designed by men, run by men, and operated to protect men from the consequences of their violence against women.

Law Enforcement Failures

Even when laws changed, enforcement lagged. Police officers, trained to view rape accusations with skepticism, often discouraged women from filing reports. Prosecutors, evaluating cases based on likelihood of conviction, declined to pursue charges when they doubted juries would believe the victim. Rape kits—evidence collected from victims' bodies—sat untested in police storage for years, sometimes decades.

The statistics are stark. The vast majority of rapes are never reported to police. Of those reported, only a small fraction result in arrest. Of those arrested, only a small fraction are prosecuted. Of those prosecuted, only a small fraction are convicted. The result is that most rapists face no legal consequences whatsoever.

The Courts and Sexual Harassment

The legal system has also failed to adequately address sexual harassment. Although Title VII prohibits harassment, proving a claim is difficult. Victims must show that the harassment was "severe or pervasive" enough to create a hostile work environment—a standard that often excludes the kind of ongoing, lower-level harassment that makes many women's working lives miserable. They must navigate complex procedural requirements, often face retaliation, and rarely receive meaningful compensation.

Employers have responded to harassment law primarily by protecting themselves from liability, not by protecting employees from harassment. Mandatory arbitration clauses prevent many claims from ever reaching court. Non-disclosure agreements silence victims and protect serial harassers. The legal system offers theoretical protections that often fail to translate into actual safety.

THE DEVIL thus fulfills his role in the politics of sexual violence through legal structures that protected rapists (resistance requirements, corroboration requirements, marital exemptions, sexual history admissibility), enforcement failures (police skepticism, prosecutorial reluctance, untested rape kits, low conviction rates), and inadequate harassment remedies (high legal standards, mandatory arbitration, non-disclosure agreements).

• • •

Evidence for the Prosecution: MAN

Individual men commit sexual violence. Individual men benefit from systems that allow such violence to go unpunished. And individual men have organized to resist reforms that would hold them accountable.

The Perpetrators

Sexual violence is overwhelmingly committed by men. This is not a controversial statement; it is a statistical fact. The vast majority of rapes, sexual assaults, and acts of sexual harassment are perpetrated by men against women. While men can be victims and women can be perpetrators, the gendered pattern is unmistakable.

Many perpetrators are not strangers but men known to their victims—dates, boyfriends, husbands, colleagues, supervisors. They use their relationships, their positions, their physical strength, and their social power to coerce sex from women who do not want it. And they rely on a system that will rarely hold them accountable.

The #MeToo revelations exposed serial predators in every industry: entertainment, media, politics, business, academia, religion. Men like Harvey Weinstein operated for decades, assaulting dozens of women, protected by their power and by the silence they could enforce through intimidation and non-disclosure agreements. These were not isolated incidents; they were patterns of behavior enabled by systems designed to protect powerful men.

The Resistance

Men have organized to resist reforms that would increase accountability for sexual violence. They have argued against rape shield laws (claiming defendants' rights to confront accusers). They have opposed expansions of harassment law (claiming due process concerns). They have attacked the #MeToo movement (claiming it has "gone too far" and creates "witch hunts").

The concern for due process is selective. The same men who worry about false accusations rarely worry about the far more common problem of true accusations that never result in consequences. The same men who claim #MeToo has "gone too far" rarely specify what the appropriate distance would be. The rhetoric of fairness masks a desire to preserve male impunity.

MAN thus fulfills his role in the politics of sexual violence through direct perpetration (the overwhelming majority of sexual violence is committed by men), enabled impunity (systems that protect perpetrators were designed by and for men), and organized resistance (opposition to reforms that would increase accountability).

• • •

The #MeToo Moment

In 2006, a Black woman named Tarana Burke created the phrase "Me Too" to help survivors of sexual abuse find solidarity through shared experience. Her work focused primarily on young women of color—those least likely to be believed, least likely to receive justice.

In October 2017, the phrase went viral. Following the exposure of Harvey Weinstein's decades of sexual predation, actress Alyssa Milano encouraged women to respond with "me too" if they had experienced sexual harassment or assault. Within hours, tens of thousands responded. Within days, millions. The hashtag spread globally, translated into dozens of languages, triggering what some called a "national reckoning" with sexual violence.

The #MeToo movement brought down powerful men in entertainment, media, politics, and business. It surfaced stories that had been suppressed for decades through shame, fear, and legal agreements. It demonstrated the sheer scale of the problem—the ubiquity of harassment and assault that women had always known but that many men claimed to find surprising.

Limits and Backlash

The movement also revealed persistent limitations. The women whose stories received the most attention were disproportionately white, wealthy, and famous. Tarana Burke's original vision—centered on the most marginalized women—was sometimes overshadowed by Hollywood celebrities. Low-wage workers, immigrant women, women of color continued to face harassment with fewer resources and less visibility.

The backlash was swift. Critics claimed the movement encouraged "rush to judgment" and "cancel culture." They worried about false accusations and ruined careers—rarely acknowledging that false accusations are rare while actual harassment is endemic. They argued that #MeToo had "gone too far" without specifying how far was appropriate or acknowledging how far it had failed to go.

Some consequences proved fragile. Harvey Weinstein was convicted in New York in 2020 and sentenced to twenty-three years in prison. In 2024, that conviction was overturned on procedural grounds. He remains subject to a separate California conviction, but the reversal demonstrated how vulnerable even the most prominent #MeToo victories could be.

• • •

Progress and Its Limits

The legal landscape around sexual violence has changed dramatically over the past fifty years. Most states have reformed their rape laws, eliminating resistance requirements, corroboration requirements, and blanket admissibility of sexual history. Marital rape is technically illegal everywhere. Sexual harassment is recognized as discrimination. These are real achievements, won through sustained feminist organizing and advocacy.

But structural change has been limited. Sexual violence remains endemic. Reporting rates remain low. Conviction rates remain lower. Harassment persists in every industry despite decades of training and policy. The culture of disbelief that Anita Hill faced in 1991 persists, as Christine Blasey Ford discovered when she testified against Brett Kavanaugh in 2018.

The Masculine Triad adapts. When legal reforms make explicit victim-blaming harder, subtler forms emerge. When high-profile perpetrators face consequences, systems develop to protect others. When movements like #MeToo create pressure for change, backlash mobilizes to contain that pressure.

The fight against sexual violence is not merely a fight to change laws, though legal change matters. It is a fight to change the assumptions embedded in culture—the assumption that women's bodies are available for male use, that women's refusals are negotiable, that women's testimony is inherently suspect. These assumptions have been encoded in law for millennia. They do not disappear because statutes change.

Progress is real but incomplete. Each generation of women inherits both the victories and the unfinished struggles of those who came before. The Masculine Triad does not surrender; it retreats, regroups, adapts. And women—naming their experiences, demanding accountability, refusing to be silent—continue to push against structures that have endured for thousands of years.

CHAPTER SEVENTEEN

The Economics of Inequality

The prosecution presents evidence of economic subjugation. While legal equality has been achieved on paper, the Triad maintains women's subordination through structural mechanisms: the wage gap, the motherhood penalty, the devaluation of feminized labor, and the exploitation of unpaid work. The evidence will show that economic inequality is not a market failure but a Triad success.

In 1963, President John F. Kennedy signed the Equal Pay Act into law, making it illegal to pay men and women different wages for substantially equal work. At the time, women working full-time earned approximately fifty-nine cents for every dollar earned by men. The gap was so stark, so obviously unjust, that legislation to address it seemed both necessary and sufficient.

More than sixty years later, women working full-time still earn only about eighty-four cents for every dollar earned by men. At the rate of progress since 1963, women will not achieve pay parity until approximately 2056—nearly a century after the law was supposed to guarantee equal pay. For women of color, the timeline is even longer. Latina women earn approximately fifty-seven cents to the white male dollar; Black women earn approximately sixty-seven cents. At current rates, Latina women will not achieve pay parity until well into the twenty-second century.

The persistence of the wage gap despite decades of legal prohibition reveals a fundamental truth: economic inequality between the sexes is not merely a matter of explicit discrimination that can be legislated away. It is embedded in the structure of work, the organization of families, the distribution of unpaid labor, and the assumptions that shape how we value different kinds of contribution. The Masculine Triad operates in the economic sphere not primarily through direct prohibition—though that too—but through a complex architecture that systematically advantages men and disadvantages women.

• • •

The Wage Gap and Its Explanations

The gender wage gap is not a single phenomenon but a composite of multiple forms of inequality, each with its own dynamics and explanations. Some of the gap reflects overt discrimination: employers who pay women less than men for identical work. Some reflects occupational segregation: the concentration of women in lower-paying jobs and industries. Some reflects the "motherhood penalty": the career costs women pay for having children. And some reflects the devaluation of work that women do—the systematic underpricing of labor performed predominantly by women.

Direct Discrimination

The Equal Pay Act and Title VII of the Civil Rights Act prohibit paying women less than men for the same work. Yet such discrimination continues. Studies sending identical resumes with male and female names to employers consistently find that applicants with female names receive lower salary offers. Audit studies reveal that employers evaluate mothers as less competent and less committed than non-mothers with identical qualifications, and recommend hiring them at lower salaries. The law may prohibit discrimination, but enforcement is difficult, and much discrimination occurs in ways that are hard to detect and prove.

Moreover, the legal standard of "equal pay for equal work" has a significant limitation: it requires comparison within the same establishment. If an employer segregates men and women into different job categories, different shifts, or different locations, it can pay them differently without technically violating the law. The law addresses the symptom but not the underlying structure.

Occupational Segregation

Women and men are not distributed randomly across occupations. Women are concentrated in education, healthcare, social work, administrative support, and service industries—sectors that pay less than the male-dominated fields of finance, technology, construction, and manufacturing. This occupational segregation accounts for a significant portion of the wage gap.

The question is why this segregation exists and why it matters. Some argue that women freely choose lower-paying occupations because they prefer more flexible hours, less physically demanding work, or jobs that align with their values. Others point out that these "choices" are constrained by socialization, discrimination, and hostile work environments that push women out of certain fields. And the devaluation of female-dominated occupations is itself suspect: when women enter a field in large numbers, wages tend to fall; when men enter, wages tend to rise. The work hasn't changed, only who does it.

The Unexplained Gap

Economists attempting to explain the wage gap control for education, experience, occupation, industry, hours worked, and other measurable factors. After these adjustments, a significant portion of the gap remains unexplained—typically around 38 percent. This unexplained gap is often attributed to discrimination, though it may also reflect unmeasured differences in qualifications or preferences.

But the distinction between "explained" and "unexplained" portions of the gap may obscure as much as it reveals. If women are steered toward lower-paying occupations by socialization and discrimination, the occupational component of the gap is not innocent—it too reflects discrimination, just at an earlier stage. If women accumulate less work experience because they are expected to perform unpaid caregiving, this too reflects systemic disadvantage. The "explained" portions of the gap are not necessarily legitimate; they may simply be forms of discrimination that are easier to see.

• • •

The Second Shift

In 1989, sociologist Arlie Hochschild published *The Second Shift*, documenting a phenomenon that working women had long experienced: the double day. Women who worked full-time in the paid labor force came home to a "second shift" of unpaid domestic labor—cooking, cleaning, childcare, household management—that their husbands largely did not share. Hochschild estimated that women worked roughly a month more per year than men when paid and unpaid labor were combined.

Decades later, the second shift persists. Women spend an average of 12.6 hours per week on housework, compared to 5.7 hours for men. Women spend more than twice as much time as men caring for children. Combined, women perform roughly 2.2 times as much unpaid household and caregiving labor as men. Even among couples where both partners work full-time, women do significantly more domestic work.

The Economic Value of Unpaid Labor

Unpaid domestic labor is economically valuable. Someone must cook meals, clean homes, care for children, manage households. If these tasks were not performed by family members, they would have to be purchased in the market. Estimates suggest that if unpaid domestic labor were included in GDP calculations, it would add approximately 26 percent to measured economic output.

Yet this labor is systematically devalued. It is performed disproportionately by women, is unpaid, is not counted in economic statistics, and confers no retirement benefits, no unemployment insurance, no worker protections. Women who perform this labor full-time are economically dependent on partners; if relationships end, they have no savings, no pension credits, no employment history. Women who perform this labor in addition to paid work have less time for career advancement, less energy for professional development, and less freedom to pursue opportunities that require long hours or travel.

The Third Shift: Cognitive Labor

Beyond physical household tasks lies what researchers call "cognitive labor"—the mental work of managing a household. Anticipating needs. Keeping track of appointments, deadlines, and obligations. Knowing when supplies need to be replenished, when bills need to be paid, when children need to be picked up. Planning meals, coordinating schedules, remembering birthdays. This invisible labor is exhausting and falls disproportionately on women.

Studies find that women take on a disproportionate share of cognitive labor even when physical tasks are more equally divided. This mental load creates emotional exhaustion that spills over into the workplace, affecting women's career trajectories and contributing to higher turnover and lower career resilience. The work is invisible, undervalued, and rarely acknowledged—yet it is essential to household functioning.

• • •

The Motherhood Penalty

No single factor affects women's economic outcomes more dramatically than motherhood. Mothers earn less than non-mothers, less than fathers, and less than they themselves would have earned had they not had children. Research suggests that the motherhood penalty accounts for nearly 80 percent of the gender wage gap. It is, in many ways, the central mechanism through which economic inequality between the sexes is reproduced.

The Dimensions of Penalty

The motherhood penalty operates on multiple dimensions. Mothers are less likely to be hired than non-mothers with identical qualifications. When hired, they are offered lower salaries. They are perceived as less competent and less committed to their jobs, even when their actual performance is identical to that of non-mothers. They are promoted less frequently and receive smaller raises. Each child under five is estimated to reduce a mother's earnings by approximately 15 percent.

The penalty varies by number of children, timing of childbearing, and socioeconomic status. Women who have children earlier and have more children pay larger penalties. Low-income mothers face larger penalties than high-income mothers—those who can least afford economic disadvantage are most disadvantaged. Black women and Latina women face penalties compounded by racial discrimination.

Crucially, fathers face no comparable penalty. In fact, they often receive a "fatherhood bonus"—higher earnings and better evaluations than childless men. The same event—becoming a parent—enhances men's economic prospects while damaging women's. The asymmetry reveals that the penalty is not about parenthood per se but about assumptions regarding who bears caregiving responsibilities.

Employer Discrimination

Some of the motherhood penalty reflects employer discrimination. Experiments sending identical resumes with and without signals of motherhood find that mothers are significantly less likely to be called for interviews and are recommended for lower salaries. Employers assume mothers will be less committed, less available, and more likely to leave. These assumptions become self-fulfilling: if mothers are denied opportunities, their careers will indeed lag.

The discrimination persists even when mothers demonstrate competence and commitment. Studies show that when mothers perform at the same level as non-mothers, they are still rated as less competent and held to higher standards. The penalty is not based on actual performance differences but on stereotyped assumptions about what mothers are like and what they will do.

Structural Factors

Not all of the motherhood penalty reflects discrimination in the narrow sense. Some reflects the reality that mothers, more than fathers, adjust their work lives to accommodate caregiving. They take more time off after children are born. They are more likely to work part-time, to choose jobs with flexible hours, to decline opportunities that require travel or unpredictable schedules. These choices carry economic costs.

But are they really choices? If childcare is prohibitively expensive or unavailable, if workplaces offer no flexibility, if fathers do not share equally in caregiving, then mothers' "choices" are heavily constrained. Women do not choose to be primary caregivers in a vacuum; they are shaped by policies, structures, and expectations that assume women will be primary caregivers. The United States offers no guaranteed paid family leave, has the highest childcare costs in the developed world, and structures workplaces around the assumption of an ideal worker unencumbered by caregiving responsibilities. Under these conditions, mothers' decisions to reduce work hours or take career breaks are less free choices than constrained responses to impossible circumstances.

• • •

Evidence for the Prosecution: GOD

Ideological justifications for economic inequality between the sexes draw on familiar themes: natural differences, complementary roles, and the special calling of motherhood. These arguments frame inequality not as injustice but as appropriate recognition of men's and women's different contributions.

The Ideology of Separate Spheres

The doctrine of separate spheres, examined in earlier chapters, assigned men to the public world of work and women to the private world of home. Though formally discredited, its assumptions persist. Women who pursue careers are suspected of neglecting their families. Women who stay home are valued in rhetoric but economically vulnerable in practice. The ideology provides a framework within which women's economic disadvantage appears natural rather than constructed.

Religious teachings reinforce this framework. Women are called to nurture; men are called to provide. Women's fulfillment comes through family; men's through achievement. These claims present economic inequality as divinely ordained role differentiation rather than human-created hierarchy. If women earn less because they prioritize family, this is fulfillment of their nature, not evidence of injustice.

The "Choices" Narrative

Contemporary defenders of the wage gap often appeal to "choice." Women choose lower-paying occupations. Women choose to work fewer hours. Women choose to take career breaks for children. These choices, the argument goes, reflect women's preferences, not discrimination. The wage gap is not a problem to be solved but a reflection of differences in values and priorities.

This narrative obscures the conditions under which choices are made. It treats socialization as irrelevant, structural constraints as nonexistent, and preferences as formed in a vacuum. It ignores that women are steered toward certain occupations from childhood, that hostile work environments push them out of others, that the absence of childcare and parental leave forces impossible trade-offs. Most fundamentally, it ignores that women's choices are made within a system designed around the assumption that men's choices are the default.

GOD thus fulfills his role in economic inequality by providing ideological justification (separate spheres, complementary roles), religious authority (women as nurturers, men as providers), and naturalization of inequality (the "choices" narrative that presents structural disadvantage as preference).

• • •

Evidence for the Prosecution: THE DEVIL

The machinery of the state—laws, regulations, policies—has both created and perpetuated women's economic disadvantage. While some laws have addressed discrimination, structural policies continue to disadvantage women in ways that appear neutral but are deeply gendered.

The Limits of Anti-Discrimination Law

The Equal Pay Act and Title VII prohibit wage discrimination, but their effectiveness is limited. The requirement that comparison be made within the same establishment allows employers to segregate workers and pay differently. The burden of proof falls on plaintiffs, who must demonstrate discrimination that employers can easily disguise. Enforcement resources are limited; the EEOC receives far more complaints than it can investigate.

Moreover, anti-discrimination law addresses only one dimension of economic inequality. It cannot address occupational segregation, cannot mandate childcare, cannot require paid leave, cannot redistribute domestic labor. The law treats symptoms while leaving structural causes intact.

The Absence of Family Policy

The United States stands almost alone among developed nations in providing no guaranteed paid family leave. When children are born, American mothers must rely on employer generosity, state programs that exist in only a few states, or unpaid leave that many cannot afford to take. This absence of policy forces women to choose between economic security and caregiving—a choice men are rarely forced to make.

American childcare is similarly inadequate. Costs are among the highest in the developed world, often exceeding rent or mortgage payments. Quality care is scarce in many areas, creating "childcare deserts" where families have few options. For many mothers, the cost of childcare exceeds what they could earn in the workforce, making employment economically irrational even when desired. These policy failures are not accidental; they reflect choices to leave caregiving to families rather than to support it publicly. And because women are expected to perform caregiving, the burden of inadequate policy falls primarily on them.

Workplace Structures

Workplaces are structured around an ideal worker who has no caregiving responsibilities—or, more precisely, who has a wife at home managing those responsibilities. The worker who can work long hours, travel at short notice, be available evenings and weekends, and prioritize work above all else is rewarded. The worker who cannot meet these expectations—typically, the worker with caregiving responsibilities—is penalized.

This structure is not neutral. It was designed around male life patterns and male expectations at a time when women were largely excluded from the workforce. It continues to privilege those (mostly men) whose lives conform to this pattern and to disadvantage those (mostly women) whose lives include caregiving. The penalty for caregiving is built into the structure of work itself.

THE DEVIL thus fulfills his role in economic inequality through limited anti-discrimination enforcement, absence of family policy (no paid leave, inadequate childcare), and workplace structures designed around male life patterns that penalize caregiving.

• • •

Evidence for the Prosecution: MAN

Individual men benefit from women's economic disadvantage and perpetuate it through their actions and inactions. They benefit from the wage gap, which gives them more money for the same work. They benefit from unpaid domestic labor, which provides them with services they do not reciprocate. And they benefit from structures that limit women's competition for positions and resources.

The Domestic Labor Gap

Men could eliminate the second shift by performing equal shares of domestic labor. They do not. Even in households where both partners work full-time, men perform significantly less housework and childcare than women. The gap begins as soon as men and women form households and widens when children arrive. It persists even when women earn more than their male partners, even when women work longer paid hours, even when couples profess egalitarian values.

The failure to share domestic labor is not merely a private matter. It has profound economic consequences. Women who perform the second shift have less time and energy for career advancement. They are more likely to reduce work hours, decline promotions, or exit the workforce entirely. Men who do not perform domestic labor are freed to devote themselves to careers, accumulating advantages that compound over time. The domestic labor gap is a mechanism through which economic inequality is reproduced within families.

The Fatherhood Bonus

When men become fathers, their earnings typically increase. Employers view them as more committed, more stable, more responsible. The same event that damages women's careers enhances men's. This fatherhood bonus reflects assumptions that fathers will not be primary caregivers—that becoming a parent will intensify men's commitment to work rather than divert it. These assumptions are often correct, because mothers pick up the caregiving slack. Men's economic advantage is thus built on women's economic sacrifice.

Resistance to Change

Men have resisted policies that would equalize women's economic position. They have opposed comparable worth initiatives that would raise wages in female-dominated occupations. They have resisted paid family leave policies that would make it easier for men to share caregiving. They have declined to take parental leave even when it is available, reinforcing expectations that caregiving is women's responsibility. Individual men may be sympathetic to equality in the abstract, but their concrete actions often preserve their advantages.

MAN thus fulfills his role in economic inequality through failure to share domestic labor (perpetuating the second shift), capturing the fatherhood bonus (benefiting economically from parenthood while women suffer), and resistance to structural change (opposing policies that would equalize women's position).

• • •

The Architecture of Disadvantage

Women's economic inequality is not a single problem but an interlocking system of disadvantages that reinforce each other. Lower wages make it economically rational for women to reduce work hours when childcare is needed. Reduced work hours lead to lower wages and fewer advancement opportunities. Fewer opportunities lead women to invest less in education and training. Less investment leads to occupational segregation. Segregation leads to lower wages. Each element of the system supports and reproduces the others.

This architecture was not designed by any single actor, but it serves the interests of the Masculine Triad. It provides cheap domestic labor for individual men. It limits women's competition for jobs, promotions, and economic resources. It keeps women economically dependent, which has consequences for their bargaining power in relationships, their ability to leave abusive situations, and their economic security in old age.

Breaking the cycle requires intervening at multiple points simultaneously. Eliminating wage discrimination is necessary but not sufficient. Providing affordable childcare is necessary but not sufficient. Mandating paid family leave is necessary but not sufficient. Changing cultural expectations about who does caregiving is necessary but not sufficient. Each intervention helps, but none alone can dismantle an architecture built over centuries.

The economic case for equality is strong. Economies grow when they utilize all their talent. Companies perform better when they draw on diverse perspectives. Families are more secure when both partners have earning capacity. But the economic case has always been strong. The question is not whether equality would be efficient but whether those who benefit from inequality are willing to relinquish their advantages.

The Masculine Triad has proven remarkably adaptable in the economic sphere. When explicit wage discrimination became illegal, it shifted to occupational segregation. When women entered male-dominated professions, it intensified the motherhood penalty. When the ideology of separate spheres lost credibility, it replaced it with the rhetoric of choice. The forms of disadvantage change; the fact of disadvantage persists.

Women have made enormous economic progress over the past century. They have entered the workforce, entered the professions, entered positions of leadership that would have been unimaginable to their grandmothers. But full economic equality remains elusive—not because it is impossible, not because women lack ability or ambition, but because the architecture of disadvantage continues to function, adapting to each challenge, finding new ways to preserve old hierarchies. The work of dismantling it continues.

CHAPTER EIGHTEEN

The Adaptable Triad

Members of the jury, we now present our final chapter of evidence. The prosecution has documented the Masculine Triad's operations across four thousand years, from Eden to the present day. But the Triad's most dangerous characteristic is not its history—it is its adaptability. Watch as GOD, THE DEVIL, and MAN transform themselves for a new era, proving that the fight for female freedom remains as urgent today as ever.

In 1991, journalist Susan Faludi published *Backlash: The Undeclared War Against American Women*, documenting a systematic effort to roll back feminist gains of the 1970s. Through media, politics, and popular culture, Faludi argued, women were being told that feminism had failed them—that their unhappiness stemmed not from persistent inequality but from having wanted equality in the first place. The cure for women's problems was a return to traditional roles.

Thirty years later, the backlash Faludi described has not abated; it has intensified and transformed. The overturning of Roe v. Wade. The rise of explicitly anti-feminist political movements across the globe. The emergence of online communities dedicated to the proposition that men are the true victims of modern society and that feminism is responsible for their suffering. The election to the American presidency of a man who bragged about sexual assault. A quarter of countries now report organized backlash against feminism and gender equality.

What we are witnessing is not simply reaction to feminist progress. It is the Masculine Triad adapting to changed circumstances, finding new forms through which to reassert old hierarchies. The Triad has always been adaptable. When divine right lost credibility, it found new ideological justifications. When explicit legal subordination became untenable, it developed subtler mechanisms. When old arguments failed, it invented new ones. This capacity for adaptation is perhaps the Triad's most dangerous feature. It does not die; it transforms.

• • •

The Manosphere

In the dark corners of the internet, a new form of organized misogyny has emerged. The "manosphere" encompasses a sprawling network of websites, forums, social media accounts, and influencers united by hostility to feminism and, frequently, to women themselves. Its various subcultures—men's rights activists, pickup artists, incels, Men Going Their Own Way—differ in their specific obsessions but share a common conviction: that men are the true victims of contemporary society, that feminism has gone too far, and that women wield illegitimate power over men.

The Language of Victimhood

The manosphere has developed an elaborate vocabulary to express its worldview. Men who accept its premises have been "red-pilled"—a reference to *The Matrix,* in which swallowing the red pill reveals the true nature of reality hidden behind comfortable illusions. The reality thus revealed is that feminism has "brainwashed" society into oppressing men while falsely claiming that women are oppressed. Feminist gains are not progress toward equality but a power grab that has left men dispossessed.

Men are categorized into hierarchies: "alpha males" who dominate women and other men; "beta males" who meekly accept their subordination; and, at the bottom, "incels"—involuntary celibates who are denied romantic and sexual relationships by women's excessive standards. Women, in this framework, are shallow creatures who mate only with the most dominant men (the "80-20 rule" holds that 80 percent of women pursue only the top 20 percent of men), leaving ordinary men celibate and humiliated.

This is, of course, a reversal of reality. Men continue to dominate positions of power in politics, business, and most other spheres of life. The gender wage gap persists. Women remain far more likely than men to be victims of sexual violence. But the manosphere has constructed an alternative reality in which these facts are either false or irrelevant, and in which the true victims are men whose natural dominance has been stripped away by feminist conspiracy.

From Online to Offline Violence

The manosphere has produced real-world violence. In 2014, Elliot Rodger killed six people and injured fourteen in Santa Barbara, California, after posting a manifesto explaining that he was "punishing women" for refusing to have sex with him. In 2018, Alek Minassian drove a van into pedestrians in Toronto, killing eleven, after posting a message hailing "the Incel Rebellion." These attacks are not isolated incidents but expressions of an ideology that treats male entitlement to women's bodies as natural and female refusal as justification for violence.

Canadian security services now classify violent misogyny as a form of ideological extremism. Researchers have documented pathways from manosphere content to radicalization, as algorithms feed users increasingly extreme material. A young man searching for fitness advice may be recommended content about "self-improvement," which leads to content about dating strategies, which leads to content about women's supposed manipulation of men, which leads to content celebrating violence against women. The radicalization pipeline operates largely outside parental awareness, on platforms designed to maximize engagement regardless of content.

• • •

Political Backlash

The manosphere represents the extreme edge of a broader political phenomenon: the incorporation of anti-feminism into mainstream politics. Across the globe, political parties have discovered that opposition to feminist gains can mobilize voters, particularly men who feel threatened by social change.

The New Traditionalism

In the United States, the Republican Party has moved from rhetorical support for gender equality to explicit opposition. The overturning of Roe v. Wade was the culmination of a decades-long strategy to capture the courts and reverse feminist legal victories. State legislatures have passed hundreds of laws restricting abortion and targeting gender studies programs in universities. The language of "traditional values" and "family" serves as cover for policies that restrict women's autonomy and reinforce male authority.

Similar patterns appear across Europe. Hungary has suppressed gender studies programs entirely, replacing them with "family studies." Italy, Poland, and other countries have seen the rise of parties that combine nationalism with explicit opposition to feminist and goals. The Istanbul Convention, a treaty on gender-based violence, has been abandoned by several signatories. Women's ministries have been defunded or had their mandates diluted.

This political backlash is often framed in the language of protecting men and families rather than attacking women. Politicians speak of a "crisis of masculinity" in which men have been displaced by feminist overreach. They promise to restore natural order, to protect families from ideological intrusion, to defend traditional values against progressive assault. The rhetoric obscures but does not change the effect: the reassertion of male authority and the restriction of female autonomy.

The Gender Divide

Political surveys reveal a widening gap between young men and young women. In many countries, women aged 18-30 lean significantly more progressive than men of the same age—a reversal of historical patterns in which age rather than gender predicted political orientation. Young men are increasingly drawn to anti-feminist parties and figures; young women overwhelmingly support progressive politics.

This divergence reflects different experiences of the same social changes. Young women have benefited from expanded educational and professional opportunities; they are more likely than previous generations to pursue higher education and careers. Young men, meanwhile, face economic precarity—declining wages, unstable employment, rising costs—that the manosphere and anti-feminist politicians attribute to feminist conspiracy rather than to economic structures. The genuine grievances of young men are channeled toward misogyny rather than toward critique of the systems that actually produce their difficulties.

. . .

The Triad Adapts

The contemporary backlash against feminism represents the latest adaptation of the Masculine Triad to changed circumstances. Its three elements continue to operate, though in forms appropriate to the present moment.

GOD: *The New Ideologies*

The ideological component of the Triad has adapted from explicit religious justification to a blend of pseudo-science, evolutionary psychology, and victimhood narrative. The manosphere invokes "biology" to naturalize male dominance—claims about evolutionary imperatives, about hardwired differences between the sexes, about the natural order that feminism has disrupted. These claims are dressed in scientific language but lack scientific foundation; they are ideology masquerading as fact.

The victimhood narrative is particularly significant. Traditional patriarchal ideology positioned men as protectors and providers, superior beings whose dominance was deserved. The new ideology positions men as victims—of feminism, of changing norms, of women who wield illegitimate power. This inversion serves multiple purposes:

it deflects criticism by claiming victimhood status, it provides a grievance around which to mobilize, and it justifies hostility toward women as self-defense rather than aggression.

Religious traditionalism has not disappeared but has formed alliances with secular anti-feminism. Evangelical Christians, Catholic conservatives, and anti-feminist secularists find common ground in opposition to reproductive rights, and gender theory. The "unholy alliance" combines religious authority with political organization, funding networks, and media presence to form a powerful opposition to feminist progress.

Evidence for the Prosecution: GOD has adapted His ideological function from explicit divine command to pseudo-scientific justification and victimhood narrative. The content changes; the function remains: providing intellectual cover for male dominance and female subordination.

THE DEVIL: Institutional Capture

The legal and political machinery of the Triad has adapted to new circumstances. Having largely lost the ability to maintain explicit legal discrimination, anti-feminist forces have pursued institutional capture: placing sympathetic judges in courts, electing sympathetic legislators to statehouses, defunding agencies that enforce anti-discrimination law.

The overturning of Roe v. Wade demonstrated the power of this strategy. For decades, anti-abortion activists worked to reshape the federal judiciary, to elect presidents who would appoint conservative judges, to confirm those judges through a cooperative Senate. The result was a Supreme Court willing to overturn a fifty-year-old precedent protecting reproductive rights—the first time the Court had removed a fundamental right. Similar strategies target other feminist achievements, from contraception access to workplace discrimination protection.

At the state level, legislatures controlled by anti-feminist majorities have passed laws restricting abortion and limiting what can be taught in schools about gender and sexuality. These laws often operate through novel mechanisms—private enforcement, bounty systems, deliberately vague standards—designed to survive judicial review while chilling the exercise of rights.

> ***Evidence for the Prosecution****: THE DEVIL has adapted His institutional function from explicit legal subordination to institutional capture and subtle mechanisms. Unable to maintain formal discrimination, THE DEVIL now works through judicial appointments, state legislatures, and facially neutral policies that achieve discriminatory ends.*

MAN: Individual and Collective Action

Individual men continue to enforce gender hierarchy through everyday actions: harassment, discrimination, domestic violence, the refusal to share domestic labor. But organized anti-feminism has given these individual actions ideological support and collective expression.

The manosphere provides community for men who might otherwise have kept their resentments private. It validates their grievances, provides explanatory frameworks, and connects them with others who share their views. What might have been individual frustration becomes collective identity. What might have been private complaint becomes public movement.

Online harassment campaigns demonstrate the collective power of organized misogyny. Women who speak publicly about feminism, who criticize powerful men, who simply exist in public online spaces, face coordinated attacks: floods of abusive messages, doxing, threats of rape and death. These campaigns are designed to silence women, to drive them from public discourse, to demonstrate that participation in public life has costs that men do not face. They are collective punishment for the transgression of visibility.

***Evidence for the Prosecution**: MAN has adapted His enforcement function from individual patriarchal control to organized collective action. The manosphere transforms private resentment into public movement, coordinating harassment campaigns that silence women and punish their participation in public life.*

• • •

Ancient Patterns, New Forms

The contemporary backlash against feminism is not a break with history but a continuation of patterns that have operated for millennia. The Masculine Triad has always responded to challenges by adapting its forms while preserving its essential function: the subordination of women to male authority.

When women gained suffrage, the Triad adapted by ensuring that Black women in the South would not actually be able to vote, by channeling women's political participation into acceptable forms, by developing new mechanisms of exclusion that did not require formal disenfranchisement. When women entered the workforce, the Triad adapted through occupational segregation, through the wage gap, through the motherhood penalty, through workplace harassment that made many occupations hostile to women. When explicit legal discrimination became untenable, the Triad adapted through facially neutral policies that had discriminatory effects, through privatized enforcement of gender norms, through ideological work that made inequality seem natural or chosen.

The current backlash follows this pattern. As feminist gains have accumulated—legal equality, reproductive rights, #MeToo, increased representation—the Triad has mobilized to contain and reverse them. The forms are new: online harassment, algorithmic radicalization, institutional capture. But the function is ancient: to ensure that women remain subordinate to men.

The Persistence of Hierarchy

Why does the Triad persist? Why, after millennia of feminist challenge, does it continue to adapt and survive?

One answer is that the Triad serves powerful interests. Men—particularly powerful men—benefit from women's subordination. They benefit economically, from women's unpaid labor and from reduced competition in the workplace. They benefit sexually, from access to women's bodies enforced by law, custom, and violence. They benefit psychologically, from the assurance of status and superiority. These benefits create incentives to maintain hierarchy even as the forms of hierarchy change.

Another answer is that the Triad is embedded in institutions that reproduce it automatically. Legal systems, economic structures, religious organizations, family forms—these institutions were designed under conditions of male dominance and continue to reflect those origins even when their explicit rules change. Institutional inertia ensures that equality requires constant effort while inequality reproduces itself.

A third answer is that the Triad has ideological resources that feminism lacks. It can appeal to tradition, to nature, to divine order—to the weight of how things have always been. Feminism, by contrast, must argue for change against the accumulated authority of the past. The burden of proof falls on those who challenge existing arrangements, not on those who defend them.

• • •

The Struggle Continues

The backlash against feminism is real and dangerous. Rights that seemed secure have been stripped away. Movements that seemed marginal have achieved mainstream influence. Young men are being radicalized into ideologies that treat women as enemies. The Triad is adapting, regrouping, advancing on multiple fronts.

But backlash is also a sign of progress. Opposition mobilizes when it feels threatened. The manosphere, the anti-feminist political movements, the organized attacks on reproductive rights—these are responses to feminist gains, not to feminist weakness. The Triad adapts because it must; if the old forms sufficed, adaptation would be unnecessary. The very intensity of contemporary anti-feminism testifies to what feminism has achieved.

Moreover, the majority still supports equality. Surveys consistently show that most people, including most men, support feminist goals: equal pay, reproductive rights, freedom from violence, equal opportunity. The manosphere is loud but not large; its influence exceeds its numbers because algorithms amplify extremism. Anti-feminist politicians win elections in part through voter suppression, gerrymandering, and minority rule. The backlash does not represent the will of the majority; it represents the capacity of motivated minorities to capture institutions and shape discourse.

The struggle continues because it has always continued. Every generation of women has faced opposition and made progress despite it. Every feminist victory has prompted backlash, and every backlash has been eventually overcome. The arc of history is not automatic; it bends toward justice only because people bend it. But it has bent, and continues to bend, in the direction of equality.

The Masculine Triad is adaptable, but it is not invincible. It has been forced to retreat, to change forms, to abandon positions that once seemed impregnable. It will continue to adapt, and feminism will continue to challenge it. The forms of the struggle change; the struggle itself persists. And as long as women continue to demand freedom—as they have for millennia, as they do today, as they will tomorrow—the Triad will face resistance it cannot fully overcome.

The prosecution rests its case on the contemporary Triad. The evidence shows that GOD, THE DEVIL, and MAN continue their ancient collaboration in new forms. The defense will surely argue that these are merely cultural disagreements, political differences, the natural friction of changing times. But the pattern is unmistakable. The Triad adapts because its function remains essential: the subordination of women to male authority. Four thousand years of evidence support this conclusion.

CONCLUSION

We began this inquiry with a question: Why, across vastly different cultures and centuries, have women been consistently subordinated to men? The evidence we have gathered points to an answer. What we have called the Masculine Triad—the coordinated operation of ideological authority, institutional power, and individual male action—has functioned across human history to create, maintain, and reproduce female subordination. This is not conspiracy; it is system. Not plot but pattern. The Triad operates not because men gather in secret to plan women's oppression but because structures built over millennia perpetuate themselves, because ideologies embedded in culture shape perception and behavior, because individual actions aggregate into collective outcomes.

Let us review what the evidence shows.

• • •

The Case Against GOD

Throughout history, ideological authorities—religious, philosophical, scientific—have provided justification for female subordination. These justifications have changed in form while remaining constant in function: to make male dominance appear natural, inevitable, divinely ordained, scientifically verified, or simply the way things have always been and must be.

In the ancient world, creation myths assigned women secondary status: formed from man's rib, responsible for humanity's fall, inherently inferior in reason and virtue. Greek philosophy elaborated these assumptions into systematic doctrine: Aristotle's "deformed male," Plato's reincarnation punishment, the association of femininity with matter and masculinity with form. Roman law encoded these beliefs into legal principle, making women perpetual minors under male guardianship.

Medieval Christianity intensified religious justification, constructing elaborate theologies of female sinfulness rooted in Eve's transgression. The witch trials demonstrated the lethal potential of these beliefs: tens of thousands of women executed for crimes that existed primarily in the minds of their accusers. Islam, Judaism, and other traditions developed their own frameworks for female subordination, different in specifics but similar in effect.

When religious authority weakened, science stepped forward. Victorian medicine discovered diseases—hysteria, neurasthenia—that conveniently required women to remain confined to domestic spheres. Evolutionary theory was enlisted to prove that female intellectual inferiority was biological destiny. Psychoanalysis pathologized women who rejected their assigned roles. Each era found new "objective" grounds for the same ancient conclusions.

Today, the manosphere invokes evolutionary psychology and pseudo-scientific claims about "natural" male dominance. Religious conservatives and secular anti-feminists form alliances to oppose reproductive rights and gender equality. The victimhood narrative positions men as the true oppressed class. The forms change; the function persists. GOD—ideological authority in whatever form—continues to naturalize and justify what is in fact constructed and contingent.

• • •

The Case Against THE DEVIL

Law and institutional power have been the machinery through which ideology becomes material reality. The state, the church, the legal system, the economy—these institutions have enforced female subordination with the full weight of organized social power.

We have traced this enforcement from the Code of Hammurabi, which treated women as property transferable between men, through Roman patria potestas, which gave fathers absolute authority over daughters, through medieval coverture, which extinguished married women's legal existence entirely. We have examined how English common law denied women property rights, contractual capacity, and legal personhood—disabilities that persisted in America until the nineteenth century and beyond.

We have documented the legal framework of witch trials, the institutional apparatus of the Inquisition, the laws that criminalized contraception and abortion, the statutes that excluded women from education, professions, and political participation. We have seen how rape laws were structured to make conviction nearly impossible, how marital rape was not merely unpunished but literally inconceivable under legal doctrine that defined marriage as permanent consent.

We have traced the long struggle for legal reform—the Married Women's Property Acts, the suffrage campaigns, the Equal Pay Act,

Title VII, Roe v. Wade—and we have seen how each victory was incomplete, contested, and subject to reversal. The overturning of Roe demonstrated that even constitutional rights are vulnerable when institutions are captured by those committed to hierarchy. State legislatures, captured courts, defunded enforcement agencies—THE DEVIL adapts to new circumstances while continuing to serve ancient functions.

• • •

The Case Against MAN

Individual men have enacted, enforced, and benefited from female subordination. This is not a claim that all men are villains or that men are inherently evil. It is a recognition that individual actions, shaped by ideology and enabled by institutional power, aggregate into systemic oppression.

Fathers have controlled daughters, husbands have controlled wives, employers have controlled workers, pastors have controlled congregants. Men have committed violence against women—domestic abuse, sexual assault, murder—at rates that constitute epidemic. Men have harassed women in workplaces, on streets, in online spaces. Men have refused to share domestic labor, extracting unpaid work that subsidizes their own careers. Men have benefited from wage gaps, from occupational segregation, from the motherhood penalty that enhances their own economic position.

Not every man has committed these acts, but every man exists within systems that advantage men as a class. The benefits of patriarchy are distributed unequally among men—race, class, sexuality, and other factors shape individual experience—but they are

distributed. Men who do not actively oppress women still benefit from systems that do. And some men—those who organize opposition to feminist reform, who populate the manosphere, who commit violence against women, who capture institutions to roll back women's rights—actively work to maintain and restore hierarchy.

• • •

The Interlocking System

The power of the Masculine Triad lies not in any single element but in their coordination. Ideology justifies what law enforces and individual action enacts. Institutions create the conditions within which individuals act and provide platforms for ideological dissemination. Individual actions, aggregated and normalized, become the customs that institutions codify and ideologies rationalize.

When one element of the Triad weakens, the others compensate. If religious authority loses credibility, scientific authority steps forward. If explicit legal discrimination becomes impossible, facially neutral policies achieve similar effects. If formal institutions cannot maintain hierarchy, informal enforcement—harassment, violence, social sanction—fills the gap. The Triad is resilient because it is redundant; attacking one element leaves others intact.

This interlocking quality explains why feminist progress has been so difficult and so easily reversed. Legal victories mean little if ideology continues to shape attitudes and informal practices continue to enforce hierarchy. Changed attitudes mean little if institutions remain structured to disadvantage women. Individual men committed to equality face systems designed to reward them for complicity in inequality. Comprehensive change requires attacking all three elements simultaneously—a task of immense difficulty.

• • •

The Persistence of Resistance

Yet change has occurred. The evidence we have gathered documents not only oppression but resistance. In every era, women have challenged their subordination. They have demanded education, property rights, political participation, bodily autonomy, economic independence. They have organized movements, written manifestos, brought lawsuits, won elections, changed laws, shifted cultures.

The resistance has achieved real victories. Women in most of the world can now own property, enter contracts, vote, obtain education, pursue careers, control their reproduction (though this right is under renewed attack), divorce abusive husbands, report sexual violence with some hope of being believed. These rights, now taken for granted, were denied for millennia and won through struggle. Every one of them was opposed as unnatural, dangerous, destructive of family and society. Every one of them is now recognized—by most people, if not by all—as simple justice.

The victories are incomplete. Legal equality has not produced actual equality. Rights formally guaranteed are undermined in practice.

Backlash has reversed some gains and threatens others. The wage gap persists, violence continues, the second shift remains, reproductive rights are disappearing in state after state. The Triad adapts, and the struggle continues.

But the struggle continues because women continue it. Each generation inherits both the victories of previous generations and the unfinished work they left behind. The feminists of the nineteenth century won property rights and suffrage; the feminists of the twentieth century won workplace protections and reproductive rights; the feminists of the twenty-first century face new challenges and build on what came before. The chain of resistance stretches back to the beginning of recorded history and forward into an uncertain future.

• • •

What the Evidence Demands

A prosecutor presenting a case does not merely accumulate evidence; she argues for a verdict. The evidence we have gathered demands certain conclusions.

First: Female subordination is not natural, inevitable, or divinely ordained. It is a human creation, maintained by human institutions, enforced by human actions, justified by human ideologies. What humans have created, humans can change. The claim that inequality is simply "the way things are" is itself an ideological move, designed to foreclose the possibility of transformation. The historical record shows that "the way things are" has changed repeatedly, usually because women demanded change and fought for it.

Second: The Masculine Triad is a system, not a collection of discrete problems. Addressing workplace discrimination while ignoring domestic labor distribution will not produce equality. Legal reform without cultural change will be undermined. Individual attitude change without institutional transformation will have limited effect. Feminism must be comprehensive because patriarchy is comprehensive. The Triad must be confronted as a system, not merely in its parts.

Third: Progress is possible but not guaranteed. The historical record shows both advance and retreat, victory and backlash. Rights gained can be lost; movements can be defeated; institutions can be captured. There is no arc of history that bends automatically toward justice. The arc bends because people bend it, and it bends back when they stop. Complacency is the ally of hierarchy.

Fourth: Men have a role to play. The Triad advantages men as a class, but it does not serve all men well. Rigid gender roles constrain men as well as women; violence harms boys who are taught to perpetrate it; hierarchy deprives men of the full humanity that comes from genuine equality. Moreover, men who recognize injustice have a moral obligation to oppose it. The evidence we have gathered indicts not only the men who actively maintain hierarchy but the men who passively benefit from it. Complicity is not innocence.

Fifth: The work is never finished. The Triad adapts, and feminism must adapt in response. Each generation will face new forms of old oppressions, new arguments for ancient hierarchies, new technologies through which control can be exercised and resistance organized. The struggle for women's freedom and independence did not begin with this generation and will not end with it. We are links in a chain that stretches across millennia.

• • •

The Verdict

This book has been, in form if not in setting, a prosecution. We have identified the defendants: GOD, THE DEVIL, and MAN—ideological authority, institutional power, and individual male action—operating together as the Masculine Triad. We have gathered evidence: the laws, the doctrines, the practices, the violence, the exclusions, the subordinations documented in these pages. We have traced the pattern across four thousand years of recorded history, across vastly different cultures and circumstances, finding everywhere the same fundamental structure of female subordination to male authority.

The verdict cannot be in doubt. The evidence is overwhelming. The Masculine Triad exists, has existed throughout recorded history, and continues to operate today. It has adapted to every challenge, found new forms for old functions, survived every reform. It is not invincible—the gains feminism has achieved prove that—but it is remarkably resilient. It will not disappear through neglect or good intentions. It must be actively and continuously opposed.

This book cannot issue a sentence. It cannot compel change. It can only present the evidence and argue for what the evidence shows. The sentence—the transformation of the systems we have documented— must be carried out by those who read these pages and by those who will never read them, by women who demand freedom and by men who recognize that their own humanity is diminished by hierarchy, by this generation and by generations yet to come.

The prosecution rests. The evidence is before you. What happens next depends not on what has been written here but on what will be done with it.

•••

In a courtroom, the prosecution's task ends when the evidence has been presented. But history is not a courtroom, and this book is not merely an academic exercise. Behind the evidence are real women—billions of them, across thousands of years—whose lives were constrained, whose potential was stunted, whose bodies were violated, whose freedoms were denied. They are not abstractions. They were our ancestors; they are our contemporaries; they will be our descendants, unless things change.

The woman burned as a witch in Salem or Würzburg. The girl denied education in Victorian England or contemporary Afghanistan. The wife beaten by her husband with legal impunity. The worker paid less than the man beside her doing identical work. The mother penalized for the children her employer's policies forced her to choose between career and family. The rape victim disbelieved, the harassment target silenced, the body policed and controlled.

This book has been written because these women existed and exist, because their suffering was and is real, because the systems that produced their suffering continue to operate. It has been written in the hope that naming the system—The Masculine Triad—might contribute to the ongoing work of dismantling it.

The Masculine Triad has endured for millennia. It has survived every challenge, adapted to every reform, found new forms for eternal functions. But it has never been without opposition. From the first woman who refused to accept her subordination as natural, through every struggle documented in these pages, to the women organizing and resisting today, the demand for freedom has been continuous. The Triad is powerful, but so is the refusal to submit to it.

The evidence has been presented. The argument has been made. What remains is the work—the endless, necessary, hopeful work—of building a world in which the evidence presented here will be historical curiosity rather than contemporary reality, in which daughters will read of their ancestors' oppression with the same incredulity we feel reading of slavery or feudalism, in which the Masculine Triad will be not a living system but a relic of humanity's long and painful childhood.

That world is not inevitable. It must be built. The building is done by those who refuse to accept what is as what must be—who insist, against all the weight of history and tradition and power, that women are fully human and deserve to be fully free. It is not a matter of relationship to men, but rather autonomy, the FEMALE inalienable right of self-determination and self-governance.

The prosecution rests. The work continues.